SAN DIEGO'S MOST HAUNTED

NICOLE STRICKLAND

SAN DIEGO'S MOST HAUNTED

The Historical Legacy and Paranormal Marvels of America's Finest City

4880 Lower Valley Road • Atglen, PA 19310

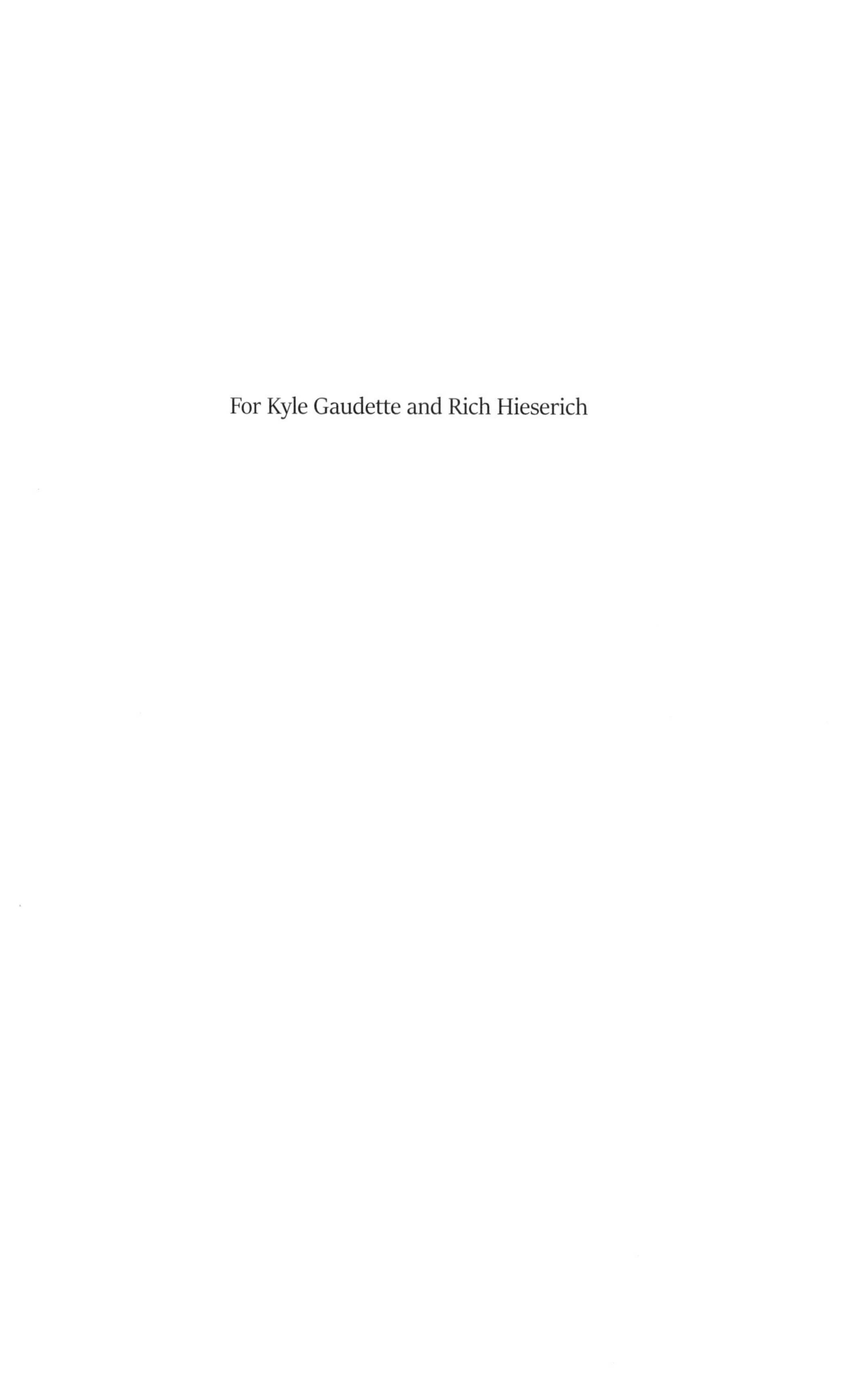

For Kyle Gaudette and Rich Hieserich

Library of Congress Control Number: 2017955198

Edited by Rachel Greene
Cover design by Brenda McCullum
Type set in Helvetica Neue, Tandelle, Sitka & Minion

ISBN: 978-0-7643-5528-8
Printed in the United States of America

Published by Schiffer Publishing, Ltd.
4880 Lower Valley Road
Atglen, PA 19310
Phone: (610) 593-1777; Fax: (610) 593-2002
E-mail: Info@schifferbooks.com
Web: www.schifferbooks.com

Do not go where the path may lead; go instead where there is no path and leave a trail.

—Ralph Waldo Emerson

CONTENTS

Foreword 12
Preface 14
Introduction 16

Part I

Chapter 1: Exploring the Paranormal 19

Part II

Chapter 2: The Historical Tapestry of San Diego, California 23
The Native Americans 25
The Spanish Period (1769–1821) 26
Mexican Period (1821–1846) 28
American Period (1846–1870) 29
New Town Arrives Again (1870–1889) 31
The Boomtown Days 32
San Diego's Contribution to the War Effort 33

Part III: Central San Diego's Most Haunted

Chapter 3: Calvary Cemetery 37
Chapter 4: Casa De Estudillo 39
Chapter 5: Cosmopolitan Hotel (Casa De Bandini) 43
Chapter 6: El Campo Santo Cemetery 50

Chapter 7: El Fandango Restaurant 53
Chapter 8: Serra Museum and Presidio Hill 56
Chapter 9: The Whaley House 65

Part IV:
Julian's Most Haunted

Chapter 10: Julian History 75
Chapter 11: The Pine Hills Lodge 78
Chapter 12: Julian Hotel 82
Chapter 13: Julian's Haven of Rest (Pioneer Cemetery) 84

Part V:
Downtown San Diego and Gaslamp Quarter District's Most Haunted

Chapter 14: Horton Grand Hotel 87
Chapter 15: William Heath Davis House
(The Davis-Horton House) 90

Part VI:
Maritime Museum of San Diego's Most Haunted

Chapter 16: B-39 Submarine 97
Chapter 17: *Berkeley* Ferryboat 100
Chapter 18: *Star of India* (*Euterpe*) 103

Part VII:
North County San Diego's Most Haunted

Chapter 19: AVO Playhouse 110
Chapter 20: Elfin Forest 116
Chapter 21: Escondido Public Library 121
Chapter 22: Rancho Guajome 125
Chapter 23: Rancho Buena Vista Adobe 128
Chapter 24: San Pasqual Battlefield 138

Part VIII:
West County San Diego's Most Haunted

Chapter 25: Del Mar Fairgrounds and Racetrack 142
Chapter 26: Hotel Del Coronado 146
Chapter 27: Hunter Steakhouse 152
Chapter 28: Twin Inns 155

Part IX:
East County San Diego's Most Haunted

Chapter 29: Buckman Springs 160
Chapter 30: Proctor Valley Road 163
Chapter 31: Santee Edgemoor Barn 165
Afterword 169

Part X: Appendices and Resources

Signs that Your Location May Be Haunted 171
What to Include in a Case Report 174
SDPRS Classes and Lectures 175
Glossary of Paranormal Terminology 176
Bibliography 181
Acknowledgments 186
About the Author 187

Foreword
"The Finest Haunts Around"

San Diego is often referred to as "America's Finest City," and one trip to this gorgeous city confirms the title is well-deserved. Just visit the amazing beaches where locals and tourists soak up the sun under blue skies, and watch as hundreds of runners, walkers, surfers, skateboarders, and cyclists show why the city also has a reputation for being one of the healthiest in the nation. Or soak up a great tourist destination like the San Diego Zoo, Sea World, the Embarcadero, or Balboa Park, all of which have gained world-famous status.

There is plenty of fine dining, not to mention hole-in-the-wall cafes and taco shops, jumping bars, cranking clubs, concert venues, Broadway shows at the Civic Theater, and cultural events that can fill up your calendar every weekend of the year. San Diego has it all.

Including ghosts.

Venture outside the city into the many surrounding towns that make up San Diego County—from the beaches, to the mountains, to the desert—and you will be surprised to learn that there are numerous places with quite a ghostly reputation indeed. In fact, local legends and creepy stories prevail, as do "regular haunts" that have become top destinations for visitors who want to experience things that go bump in the night—and we are not talking about hips in a retro '70s dance club!

Nicole Strickland knows all about these haunted places. Not only does she live in San Diego, but she is also a member of the city's finest paranormal research group and has written extensively about haunted activity, most notably about the legendary *Queen Mary*.

Now Nicole turns her attention toward this Southern California paradise, where the surf meets the turf, and where you can go from riding the waves to skiing in the mountains within the space of a two-hour drive. This book is filled with stories of spooky spaces and paranormal places. From the more well-known Hotel del Coronado and the Whaley House—featured numerous times on television travel and ghost hunting shows—to more obscure locations only those who reside here know about (and even many of them do not have a clue!), one might be very surprised to find that the finest city in America is also one of the scariest . . . that is, if you are afraid of ghosts, apparitions, and entities.

This book is chock-full of actual documented paranormal investigations and frightening personal accounts, many at recognizable historical locations that might surprise you. Nicole knows the field well and presents the information in a manner that will both educate and entertain even those of us who have lived here a while and may not be aware of the region's rich supernatural history.

I have experienced some of these strange locations here in San Diego, and I am thrilled to be a part of this intriguing book, which is sure to have me off in search of more creepy corners of the place I have called home for decades. Those of us who live in San Diego, with its gorgeous scenery, awesome and friendly people, and perfect weather, would not live anywhere else. Now we get to call it a "Paranormal Paradise" on top of everything else, and invite new interest to the places we have come to know and love, as well as those places even we locals have never heard of until this book.

How exciting it is to discover that your hometown is haunted! Come and explore the spooky side of San Diego. Learn the background behind these cool "hot" spots, and read some chilling stories of those who have been there and experienced the unexplained. Then add San Diego to your bucket list of places to visit and bring your courage. You'll need it, along with this book, for the perfect haunted holiday!

Marie D. Jones, best-selling author of *PSIence: How New Discoveries in Quantum Physics and New Science May Explain the Existence of Paranormal Phenomena*

Preface

Even though I was born in Huntington Beach, California, I will always call San Diego my hometown, as I have spent the majority of my life in this city. Even though I have had an innate intrigue in the supernatural since birth, I officially commenced my quest to investigate the unknown after the 2001 death of my beloved grandmother, Helen LoPinto.

Growing up, I was extremely close to my grandmother. She resided in the Kensington area of San Diego, approximately ten minutes from my house. As you can imagine, I was always excited to go over to "Grandma's house," whether it was after school, on the weekends, or during the holiday season. Speaking of the holidays, our family spent Christmas Eve and Christmas Day at Helen's residence every year. By talking about it here, I can almost smell the aroma of authentic Italian sausage, meatballs, and spaghetti cooking in the oven and on the stove, as it was annual celebratory cuisine at the LoPinto home.

There are so many wonderful memories I have of spending time with Helen throughout the years. As a little girl living in Las Vegas, Nevada, I can still envision my overjoyed excitement seeing Grandma and Grandpa pulling up to our home after driving from San Diego. I recall Helen reading my favorite books to me before my bedtime and us playing "Marco Polo" in our swimming pool. As a teen, I remember Helen waving her hand as we drove up to or departed from her house after a quiet afternoon gathering. Whether we visited in San Diego, Las Vegas, or at our family Welk Resort time-share, the recollections are countless and safe in my heart for eternity.

The afternoon before her peaceful passing, Helen called me; I was in my senior year of college. She called wanting to make sure I was "okay," which seemed odd to me at the moment. Now, in retrospect, I realize it was her way of making sure everything was in order prior to her departure from the mortal plane. I chatted with Helen on the phone for about fifteen minutes, not yet realizing that it would be my final phone call with her.

The following afternoon, my mom called me and I innately knew that something was not right as she echoed the words, "Sweetheart, I want you to know how much I love you . . ." It is that instinctual mother/daughter connection where no words need to be said in all actuality. With butterflies swirling in my stomach, I felt my world caving in when she continued with, ". . . but I want you to know that Grandma passed away early this morning." Tears engulfed my face as anger and sorrow filled my heart.

A few days after Helen's funeral services I started to experience odd phenomena in my apartment. It commenced with hearing the doorknobs rattle of their own volition. Let me insert here that my grandmother always checked the doors at night to make sure they were locked. Then came the disembodied caress on my face as I was studying for a midterm, a sensation that felt as if it came from someone I knew

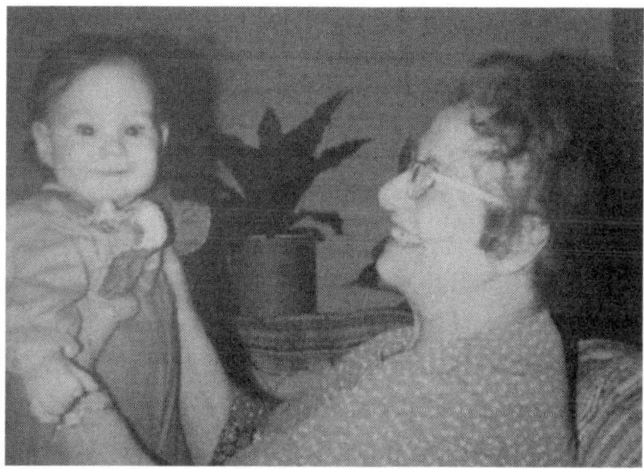

The author as a baby with her grandmother, Helen LoPinto, c. 1979.

and loved. Little did I know at the time that just a few days would pass before I would encounter one of the most profound and life-changing events: seeing Helen's spirit standing in my bedroom, about ten years younger and adorned in her favorite blue-and-white house dress. In paranormal terms she was a solid apparition, almost glowing from behind, as if she had a spotlight behind her. She appeared like this for a few nights.

I shared the above experiences with my mom, and we collectively decided to talk to Helen and let her know that the family was okay and that she was free to move on. Once we did that the experiences stopped. I strongly believe now that her spirited appearance was her way of saying goodbye, and one last grandmotherly action of ensuring that the family was okay. Today Helen does visit us from time to time; however, I know in my heart that she is at peace, having evolved to spirit.

I have always been intrigued by the paranormal, specifically ghosts and hauntings. However, the experiences I encountered with my grandmother's spirit catapulted me into actively investigating the unknown. In a way, they initiated my quest as a paranormal researcher and laid the foundation for my work in the field. In modern time, as I encounter more spiritual experiences with ghosts and spirits, I am reminded of seeing my beloved grandma in ethereal form, thanking her for giving me that ultimate experience. I further thank her for paving the way for me as a paranormal researcher and helping to instill the relentless passion I have for exploring the unknown.

The San Diego Paranormal Research Society has conducted several ghost research and investigative projects at many of the historical locations discussed in this book. Writing this book is my individual way of thanking the city's notable people and early pioneers, and thus highlighting the historical impact they have made on "America's Finest City." Additionally, I want to honor and keep history alive in the present by talking about the paranormal occurrences at these mentioned sites. In doing so, it is my hope to bridge the people of the past with those of the present. As you can conclude, this book is an interwoven tapestry of the everlasting bond between history and the paranormal.

Nicole

Introduction

Humans have always had an instinctive fascination with the concept of life after death. Since the dawn of time people have been on a quest to discover, examine, and hopefully answer the questions that exist regarding the supernatural realm: What are ghosts? How does consciousness survive death? Where exactly do we go after our physical body ceases to function? Are spirits actually communicating with us? How are they able to do so? The list of questions goes on for eternity. Many cultures exhibit some sort of belief regarding life after death. The subject of ghosts and spirits dates back many years and is discussed by people from all walks of life, ethnicities, religions, and demographics.

In recent years, the desire to study and seek out ethereal energies has grown exponentially. Perhaps there are other prevailing reasons why society is interested in ghosts and hauntings, but one aspect remains clear: The interest in studying the paranormal has infiltrated our very core of existence. Hopefully, as time goes on, we will better understand what constitutes the vast realm of the supernatural.

Historical events and paranormal phenomena share a deep kinship. They complement each other greatly. Thus, you cannot completely understand a haunting unless you examine the location's past. Thorough paranormal researchers spend time digging through historical archives, mainly to understand the story of that site's previous years and possibly explain its supernatural activity. Learning about the people and events of a location's bygone era will benefit paranormal investigators during their research project(s). You can say that the study of ghosts and hauntings is a way of piecing together the notable events of years gone by.

I have lived in San Diego the majority of my life. I was born in Huntington Beach, California, an affluent town in Orange County. After a six-year stint in Las Vegas, Nevada, my family and I moved back to California. I spent the better part of my youth in San Diego, and after graduating from high school, I attended the University of Arizona. It was during this period that I realized my love for history and writing. It was also during this time that my beloved grandmother, Helen LoPinto, passed away; just a few days after, I encountered her spirited apparitional form in my college apartment. This profound, life-changing event further ignited my intrigue in the supernatural and commenced my quest in investigating the unknown.

San Diego, California, also known as "America's Finest City," offers more than just scenic excellence, attractive weather, stunning beaches, world-renowned attractions, delectable fish tacos, etc. It is one of the most historical cities in the entire nation, if not the entire world. It is for this reason and many others why San Diego is one of the most well-known and talked about places in the nation. As the sun rises and sets each day in this southernmost California town, another page of its history book is revealed.

Introduction

With history bonded to the paranormal, it comes as no surprise that San Diego is known as one of the most haunted cities in the entire country. You can imagine that this book would well exceed thousands of pages if I mentioned every single historical aspect and talked about every single ghostly populated location. As a volume of typical length, this book gives a general overview of the city's noted time periods, as well as historical highlights of various haunted locations. Furthermore, it will share theories as to possibly why these places became paranormally rich environments, as well as discuss some of their haunted claims and encounters. If you are someone who is intrigued by San Diego history and the supernatural, then these next several pages will be a delight to read.

For many years I have been studying the paranormal and have conducted several ghost research projects at many of the historical sites mentioned in this book. In a sense, this project's mission is to connect the people of San Diego's past with those of the present. Furthermore, it is my individual way of thanking all of the city's notable people and early pioneers for their relentless efforts in establishing "America's Finest City." Ghostly occurrences and happenings are an added ingredient to the historical tapestry of San Diego, California. Discussing some of the supernatural encounters the San Diego Paranormal Research Society and others have experienced at these landmarks is a way of keeping history alive in the present.

As mentioned, I aim to highlight how paranormal phenomena exist as a method of bridging the historic chronicles of times gone by with those in the present. The olden days are alive and well in the soul of our current day, where history shares its story and whispers to us via the veils of time. This book is written from my heart and soul, and is surely my way of highlighting the major milestones of San Diego, "America's Finest City."

PART I

Chapter 1: Exploring the Paranormal

I am honored to live in a city with such a noted historical past. Every day I am reminded of the unrelenting effort and courage it took on the part of San Diego's founding fathers, people who undeniably shaped the infrastructure of "America's Finest City." Perhaps the people of its past are continuing on with their work from beyond the grave. We should pay close attention to and commend these individuals, as San Diego would not be what it is today without their contributions.

Since working with the San Diego Paranormal Research Society (SDPRS), I have conducted many historical and paranormal research projects at various noted historical locations in San Diego. I have had the privilege of learning more about many of the city's native peoples, founding fathers, and early pioneers—individuals who inherently helped shape its culture, environment, and economic platforms. For the SDPRS team, paranormal research is our way of learning about the county's past and those who walked the land before us. Writing this book is my way of recognizing and honoring these courageous men and women.

It must be said that some of the peculiar myths surrounding a historic location may not be verifiable as fact. This points out a huge responsibility for each paranormal researcher: to discover and dispel the false legends while unearthing the plausible reality for why places become haunted. Successful investigators examine a site, looking for logical and natural reasons for alleged supernatural activity. If, after extensive inspection, one cannot find a believable reason for a location's ghostly claims and events, then one can conclude that the occurrences there are indeed unexplainable.

To attempt understanding what constitutes the spiritual realm, a person must study and examine aspects of the human psyche, including its emotions, brain functions, and the communication process. There are various prevailing theories that attempt to rationally explain the causes of ghosts and spiritual energy. These are put into effect as a way to comprehend the reasons behind spiritual existence in the mortal realm, not to prove or disprove paranormal activity. The following hypotheses need to be examined—not necessarily answered—for us to connect the pieces of the supernatural puzzle:

1. The Psychokinetic Effect: Generally speaking, psychokinesis (PK) is the ability of our mind to move objects. However, I think we can apply it as a theory for the existence of paranormal phenomena. Due to the huge wave of interest in studying ghosts and hauntings, is it possible that we are psychokinetically attracting and/or causing paranormal activity?

2. The Electromagnetic Effect: Many household electrical items emit some amount of EMF (electromagnetic frequency). It is theorized that places that have an abundant amount of EMF energy are also said to be paranormally active. On the contrary, it is theorized that ghosts and spirits also release EMF, and can thus manipulate the environment's natural electromagnetic field. With the advent of technology, is society causing and/or increasing paranormal energy by using the many technological gadgets available in today's market?

3. The Cosmic Effect: I have often pondered whether or not there is a cosmic shift that has opened the door for the mortal realm to study and interact with spiritual energy. Is there some universal, yet elusive reason for us examining and communicating with ethereal beings?

4. The Historical Effect: As mentioned, history and the paranormal go together like peanut butter and jelly. History paves the foundation for spiritual activity. Could this explain why supernatural events exist in many old cities and towns?

5. The Angelic Effect: I have often wondered if angels and/or higher beings are contributing to society's overall interest in working with spiritual energy. Perhaps they are acting as liaison between the living and deceased. In a way this correlates to the cosmic effect.

Of course, there are other theoretical conjectures for the existence of ghosts and spirits. As we move through our field research, perhaps we will develop others as well. In my opinion, the more hypotheses we develop and test, the closer we will be to discovering what lies beyond the mortal realm. Even though we may inch closer to understanding, I do believe that some of what we are exploring is to remain elusive until it is our individual time to arrive at the pearly gates.

Paranormal research entails the scientific and/or metaphysical study of ghosts and hauntings. The technological aspect of today's paranormal study has evolved significantly. Today, many researchers utilize a variety of environmental monitoring equipment to examine the surroundings of an alleged haunted location. Furthermore, investigators use various audio, photo, and video equipment for documentation purposes. Intuitively inclined examiners use metaphysical tools, such as certain crystals, divining rods, and pendulums, to communicate with ethereal energies.

Various investigative methodologies are employed during a ghost research project. Utilizing environmental monitoring devices, such as electromagnetic field detectors, temperature sensors, etc., investigators examine how the environment plays into supernatural events. Researchers conduct electronic voice phenomena (EVP) sessions while utilizing assorted recording devices. An EVP capture is an anomaly that is not heard by the naked ear at the time of recording, but is heard via the playback mode. Additionally, Instrumental Trans Communication (ITC) is another investigative technique that is reserved for "real time" communication sessions with the departed. Furthermore, vigils should be done at the beginning and/or during the entire investigation project as a way to acquire a general feeling of a location.

Crucial to the overall success of the paranormal research project, each team member must follow protocols and standard operating procedures, and conduct their work in a respectful and reverent manner. Each investigator should understand his or her duties and work in a cohesive and collaborative manner. There are no experts in the field of paranormal study; rather, we are all students with the common goal of discovering what lies beyond the mortal realm.

Possessing a broad understanding of a location's storied past will enable a researcher to conduct more effective experimentation with the ethereal world. Look closely at what research-based experiments, hypotheses, and methodologies have been implemented. Educate yourself on how the various theories for paranormal research can be applied to a certain place. In addition to learning about its people(s), study the types of otherworldly claims and documented experiences. Knowing all of this and more will make for a more holistic and well-rounded investigation.

At this point it might be useful to explain that, while often used synonymously, ghosts and spirits are two different types of energies. According to *Spirited Queen Mary: Her Haunted Legend*, when a person transitions, he or she may have unfinished business in the mortal realm; thus, the person's energy remains, usually stuck in a particular place. The consensus among paranormal researchers is that a ghost is the energy of a once-living person who remains earthbound, unable to move on to the "light" for various reasons. On the other hand, spirits are the ethereal liveliness of those who have moved on peacefully, but are willfully able to come back to the living world. Spirits are not stuck in our realm, nor do they have unfinished business. Today, paranormal researchers have various methods for helping ghosts move on to where they need to go; however, some of them will choose to remain in our living world.

It is perfectly acceptable to have a healthy dose of skepticism, as it is needed to remain in an unbiased mindset. In fact, many people confuse the words skepticism and cynicism, implying their meanings are interchangeable. Skepticism enables individuals to stay balanced and approach their studies with an open mind. Skeptics may have doubt about the spirit world, but are still able to showcase a welcoming attitude toward it. In contrast, cynicism is unshakable doubt: no matter what a person experiences, he or she will most likely never believe in the spirit world.

There are numerous theories for why locations boast supernatural activity. Remember, not all sites that have ethereal occurrences are classified as being haunted, whereas all sites that are haunted do have paranormal activity. To this day, no one can definitively explain the existence of ghosts and spirits. There are relevant theories that attempt to explain the underlying reasons for supernatural energy.

As we move through our field research, perhaps we will develop other theories as well. In my opinion, the more hypotheses we develop and test, the closer we will be to discovering what lies beyond the mortal realm.

PART II

Chapter 2: The Historical Tapestry of San Diego, California

San Diego inhabits a unique place in the topography of California and the United States. It is situated in the southwestern part of the nation, with the Pacific Ocean to the west and Mexico to the south. Popular communities Riverside, Orange County, and Los Angeles lie to the north, and desert and mountain regions reside in the east.

The gradual formation of San Diego Bay and its adjacent lands occurred about 1,000,000 years. Most historians believe that the very first San Diegans were Asians who traveled in various immigrations from Siberia to Alaska 20,000 years ago. Intriguingly, Museum of Man scientists excavated a skull near the area of Del Mar in 1929, presumed to be 48,000 years old. A second group of immigrants to the region arrived about 8,000 BC. These San Dieguito peoples were nomadic hunters and gatherers from the Rocky Mountains and Sierra Nevadas. Around 3,000 BC, the ancestors of San Diego's modern-day tribes migrated to the area. The Diegueños originated from these people, eventually splitting into the Diegueño and Kumeyaay tribes.

Historians have honored Juan Rodriguez Cabrillo as the first European to have discovered San Diego Bay. In May 1602, Spain placed Don Sebastian Viscaino from Acapulco, Mexico, on an exploration assignment up the western coast. That following November, Viscaino arrived at the city's cove and named the Coronado islands in honor of his cohort, Coronado.

The exact name "San Diego" has elusive origins. Allegedly, Viscaino named the city to commemorate his flagship, known as the *San Diego*. Since early explorers held religious ceremonies on the bay's shores two days after their arrival (November 12, 1602), there may be a more accurate correlation to the official name of "America's Finest City." You see, the day these men held their services is known in Spain as the feast day of a 1400-born Spanish saint named San Diego de Alcalá. After Viscaino's first markings on the city, it would be a lengthy 166 years before another human sailed into port.

Hundreds of years ago, San Diego's five substantial rivers, along with the ocean's current flowing into the sand and silt, emptied into the Pacific Ocean. This developed into the Coronado Peninsula, ultimately leaving us with San Diego Bay. Point Loma, one of the city's southwest areas, protects the harbor. The bay's entrance consists of a thin channel in between Point Loma and North Island. The city has one of the most influential harbors in the Pacific region, which helps assist in its economic well-being. One such contributor is the fishing industry run by Italians and Portuguese, as well as the United States Navy and aircraft businesses.

San Diego is a community consisting of many residential districts, businesses, and suburban towns casing approximately one hundred square miles of beaches, canyons, and mesas. Some of the central and northern coastal districts include Mission Bay, the affluent area of La Jolla and Del Mar, Solana Beach, Carlsbad, and Oceanside. Downtown San Diego, including the Gaslamp Quarter, is situated along the eastern to southeastern gradients of the harbor. As you travel a tiny bit north, you will run into the nationally recognized Balboa Park and Mission Valley area. Other small communities north and northeast of Mission Valley include Clairemont, Kearny Mesa, Mira Mesa, Rancho Peñasquitos, Tierrasanta, Scripps Ranch, Sabre Springs, Rancho Bernardo, and Carmel Mountain. San Diego's North County consists of Poway, Escondido, Fallbrook, San Marcos, and Vista. Its southern region includes the areas National City, Chula Vista, and Eastlake. El Cajon is perhaps the largest eastern valley in the main heart of the city. Each area is distinct in its own right, but aligns with what San Diego is known for: its alluring climate, eye-catching beauty, and sense of confidence.

The city has a generally mild climate all year long. Its average mean temperature is around 61°F. There are a variety of palm and eucalyptus trees seen almost anywhere in the city. Intriguingly, San Diego County is presumed to have one of the strongest mixtures of mineral wealth. In fact, hundreds of varying types of minerals have been found. Some of these include molybdenum, Lithia, graphite, arsenic, feldspar, and precious and semiprecious gems. We know that in 1870, gold was extremely important to the mining areas; however, its production has dwindled in later years. Another interesting fact is that since 1901, more than 1.5 million dollars' worth of gems have been extracted from the county's mines. Regarding paranormal phenomena, it is theorized that certain minerals and crystals can attract spiritual energy, thus offering another plausible reason for the city's hauntings.

The 2010 census revealed that the population consisted of 3,095,313 people, making it trail behind Los Angeles as the second most densely inhabited area in California. In the Western Pacific part of the United States, San Diego is the most southern city of importance and the nation's first port of call north of the Panama Canal.

Formed on February 18, 1850, San Diego County is the birthplace of California, and is noted as having one of the nation's most geographically and historically rich environments. It is identified as one of the country's major metropolitan cities. Thousands of people come from all over the world each year to visit its many popular tourist attractions. Its climate and world-renowned beaches attract tourists on a monthly basis. People can spend their day surfing at the beach, camping or skiing in the mountains, and hiking or surveying various flowers in the desert, among many other activities. San Diego is home to many historical abodes and affluent coastal beach towns that are sure to cater to those who want a weekend getaway. It has something for everyone; perhaps this is why it has garnered the nickname "America's Finest City."

The Native Americans

The native populace who resided near what is presently known as San Diego were called the Diegueños by the Spanish people. The Hokan family lived in the extreme southern and eastern portions, including the neighboring areas of Baja, California, and Arizona. These natives were relatives of the Yuma people. The Yuman, or Hokan sub-family, included the Kumiai, which are separated into the eastern Kamia tribes and the Kumeyaay of the northern and southern regions. The Ipai were north of the San Diego River, whereas the Tipai resided in the southeastern regions. The Uto-Aztecan native tribes resided in North County. The Shoshonean sub-group arrived in the area around 1,000 years ago, including the Luiseño, Cupeño, and Cahuilla. It is estimated that as many as 20,000 indigenous people existed in the region at one time.

Sadly, these early residents were often mistreated and misunderstood. Lacking sufficient knowledge of their cultures, some folks claimed that the Native Americans were dumb, lazy, messy, and lacked morals. These dehumanizing terms were not only disrespectful, but also entirely false, as these native peoples were the epitome of creativity, ingenuity, and survival. They mastered the ability to utilize Spanish tools to assist in the construction of missions, forts, and ranch homes. These early inhabitants learned many skills in the areas of farming, agriculture, and animal husbandry. Thus, they had to get used to being around other cultivated animals.

With the arrival of the mid-eighteenth century, the majority of the area's indigenous people shared cultural traits. They possessed deep knowledge of the region's ecological platforms and were specialists in hunting and gathering survival techniques. The Native Americans lived in *rancherias*, an amassed collection of crude huts constructed out of tule grass and branches. These consisted of approximately forty sleeping quarters. Twenty such villages existed near San Diego's bay area. Sweat houses were common to the tribes of the region, where men indulged in therapeutic exercises. Tribes also utilized the river for cleaning purposes, thus attacking the notion that its residents lived in filth. Due to the city's favorable climate, most inhabitants wore very few garments. In colder months they wore items made from rabbit, otter fur, and deerskin. Tools were made of bone, shell, wood, and stone. The women were well-versed in the construction of baskets, which served many uses. For defense and hunting purposes, the natives utilized bow and arrow, as well as slings, clubs, spears, and an occasional cobblestone.

Socializing among tribe members was innately important to the native peoples of San Diego. They played many games, danced, and held village ceremonies. These rituals centered on any momentous transitional period, such as puberty, marriage, or death. Ceremonial celebrations for females took place for the preparation of marriage or having children. The males consumed jimsonweed potion as a way of envisioning future accomplishments. The elders were revered and sang songs as a way to educate the young. Religious customs primarily concerned areas of who created the gods, life after death, and supernatural powers.

Intriguingly, the Kumeyaay peoples seemed to believe in the concept of a soul. They believed that when a family member passed on he or she would go to the stars.

Tribal members often believed that spiritual energy could return to the living for various reasons, so suitable funeral rituals were performed. Individuals were cremated the day after they passed away, and the deceased individual's items were burned.

Many of the tribes subsisted on vegetation, but many varieties of protein supplemented their diet, including rabbits, squirrels, quail, ducks, crows, coyotes, and mice. They also consumed reptiles (snakes) and frogs (amphibians). Acorns were ground and cooked, providing a nice carbohydrate. Various fruits or seeds could be added to the acorns to provide extra flavor and texture. Other foods consisted of currants, wild plums, agave, and yucca. The coastal tribes subsisted on shellfish and ocean fish captured by certain nets. Mesquite beans were the main starch component for desert tribes. Much work and labor went into harvesting acorns, nuts, and beans.

The native peoples displayed unique ways of dealing with injury and illness. For example, medicine men derived several ways to cure illness, such as sucking blood from infected tissue, blowing tobacco smoke over the diseased area, or spurting saliva or water over an individual. They also specialized in massage and medicinally treating snake bites.

Physical characteristics of the tribes included a robust physique with dark brown skin, flat nose, and wide face. Many of the padres spoke about the Native Americans disparagingly; however, Father Crespí relayed that they were quite skilled at mechanics and learned Spanish right away. Furthermore, the men in Viscaino's camp relayed that the Native Americans were armed with bows and arrows but had a friendly disposition. Some of the early missionaries and soldiers felt that the native peoples were quite aggressive.

San Diego's 1860 census revealed 2,807 Native Americans resided in the area. This was not entirely accurate, as it only counted twenty-five of the forty-five tribal villages. Some were able to find low-paying jobs, but Judge Benjamin Hayes revealed that there were "too many influences now working against any sensible improvement of their condition." (James R. Mills, *San Diego: Where California Began*) In 1874, Commissioner Charles A. Wetmore visited the city and advocated for the establishment of various small reservations and the re-institution of Roman Catholic missionary work. By executive order in 1875, President Ulysses S. Grant reserved land for nine Indian reservations, including Portrero, Cahuila, Capitan Grande, Santa Ysabel, Pala, Agua Caliente, Sycuan, Inaja, and Cosmit. With the arrival of the 1880s, further land was reserved for the natives. In the late nineteenth century, special laws were approved by the federal government to assist Native Americans throughout San Diego.

The Spanish Period (1769–1821)

Point Loma was the premiere California land spotted by Juan Rodriguez Cabrillo and the Europeans. In June 1542, he sailed north from Navidad to explore the northwest coast, specifically the Straits of Anian, also referred to as the Northwest

Passage. This passageway was rumored to extend from the Atlantic to the Pacific via North America, thus establishing a convenient route for voyagers. Two of Cabrillo's vessels—the *San Salvador* and *Victoria*—were charted for this daunting task. Finally, on September 28, after a grueling 103 days at sea, Cabrillo and his men located Point Loma and Upper California, which he called San Miguel. The Spanish stayed here for six days, then traveled northward to San Miguel Island, where Cabrillo broke his leg (some accounts say he broke his arm) and later succumbed to his injury.

Later on, other men discovered the southernmost end of California. Sir Francis Drake, Sir Thomas Cavendish, and others then traveled to the Pacific Ocean in the latter part of the sixteenth century. In 1579, Drake claimed Northern California for England. On May 5, 1602, Sebastian Vizcaino, along with three ships—*San Diego*, *Santo Tomás*, and *Tres Reyes*—explored California's coast. On November 10, he landed at Point Loma after five months at sea. Two days later San Miguel was named San Diego, in honor of his flagship by the same name. Once he returned to Mexico, he recommended to New Spain's government that settlements should be established in California. Thus, he put together an expedition to California; however, his destination was changed to Rico de Oro and Rico de Plata, two mythical islands that intrigued the Spanish.

One hundred and sixty-seven years went by before men traveled into San Diego Bay. The Spanish colonization of Alta, California, began in 1769, after there were fears that the Russians would grab on to California harbors, ultimately threatening the Spanish possession of Mexico. The Spanish government sent soldiers, settlers, and missionaries to inhabit and acquire New Spain's northwestern borderlands. One of the main players in this exploration was Gen. Jose de Galvez, a Spanish representative of King Carlos III. He instituted plans to occupy Alta, California, and elected individuals who would lead these four expeditions to San Diego the same year. This entire undertaking was to be done via the founding and cohesive relationship between the presidio, mission, and pueblo.

Gaspar de Portolá, the first governor of California, and the lead commander for the colonization endeavor, was responsible for a land journey that reached San Diego Bay. Known as the "Sacred Expedition of 1769," he arrived in June, with the rest of the group arriving with Father Junípero Serra, the father of the mission system. Father Junípero Serra arrived to found a presidio, mainly serving as a medical facility. Two days after Portolá traveled northward, the Franciscan fathers—Serra, Juan Gonzalez Vizcaino, Fernando Parron, and Francisco Gomez—blessed an exact spot on the presidio and named it San Diego de Alcalá, the premiere mission in Alta, California. Eventually, the fort and mission were gradually expanded to include a settlement under Spanish and then Mexican rule.

Later during the ceremony, he also dedicated the area's premier presidio (military settlement) as a way to protect the mission. San Diego was officially founded on July 16, on a hill that boasted compelling views of Mission Valley. Known as the "Plymouth Rock of the Pacific Coast," this area signaled the beginning of European civilization in California. A chapel and an adobe church were built, and the early days primarily consisted of nursing the Spaniards who became ill. After some time they befriended the local native peoples.

During this period, approximately twenty percent of the region's native people were integrated into the mission lifestyle. Many had not developed sufficient immune systems and died as a result. Thus, neither private citizens nor any missionaries were allowed outside of the structure without a military escort. Those who survived learned various trades and developed knowledge of the Spanish language. However, relationships suffered between the Kumeyaay people and the soldiers, resulting in the building of a stockade.

By 1772, these fortifications included soldier barracks, a supply warehouse, missionary living quarters, and a chapel. Adobe bricks soon replaced the native people's original log and brush huts. Two years later, the newly founded mission was moved six miles up the river near the Kumeyaay community, Nipaguay, known today as Mission Valley. The natives from the El Capitan region rebelled and in turn burned the entire mission structure in November 1775.

In 1777, Mission San Diego was re-dedicated. Native Americans were employed to work in the gardens, orchards, fields, and ranges. Their work days commenced with a morning mass, followed by a breakfast of pozole or ground barley cooked with meat, vegetables, or occasionally chocolate. The mission system was ruled by a patriarchal hierarchy. The natives who were not yet married stayed in locked barracks, whereas married couples resided in huts. Also, corporal punishment was imposed upon those who went against the rules.

In 1812, a massive earthquake destroyed much of the mission church. The chapel was reconstructed, with church services commencing the following year. Further building continued through 1813, with community mission system establishments ensuing, such as a residential complex, corrals, courtyards, a church, workshops, agricultural facilities, gardens, and a burial ground. In 1818, the *asistencia* (mission outpost) was founded at Santa Ysabel, along with a little chapel.

A prevailing force in San Diego, the mission system had a substantial effect on all of the native peoples from the city's coastal regions to its inland locations. The San Diego Presidio historic location celebrates the development of the first European establishment on the Pacific Coast and Father Serra's first mission institution.

Mexican Period (1821–1846)

In 1821, a Mexican officer by the name Gen. Agustin de Iturbide announced that he was Emperor Agustin I of Mexico. Mexico became emancipated from Spain in 1822, causing San Diego to become part of the Mexican democracy. On April 20, 1822, the Mexican flag was hoisted over the presidio, and San Diegans affirmed their loyalty to it. In all, California was escorted into a new epoch as a Mexican dependency with the closing of the mission period. Foreign trading was then allowed, as the Mexican government opened the State of California to overseas ships.

Increased demands for hide trading resulted in an increased need for grazing lands. At the time, the yearly port income rose to $34,000 due to the growing hide trade. Animal skins were nicknamed "California Banknotes," becoming the most valuable provision for export purposes. Private land grants were soon distributed in the 1820s, by the Mexican government, thus ushering in the rancho period. The rancho system contained substantial estates used for farming. Some of the famous families of this period included the Picos, Carrillos, Bandinis, and Estudillos.

It was during the 1820s, when Old Town sprouted into existence. People were therefore optimistic about constructing their own plots outside secured walls. This was allowed by the christianization of the native peoples, along with the reduced fear of foreign attacks and the vanishing of royal dominance over the presidio. In 1829, San Diego showcased about thirty homes, mostly inhabited by retired soldiers and their families.

Much of the land was secularized in 1833, and up until 1846, the rancho system controlled life in the Golden State (California) until the American conquest that same year. During this time period San Diego witnessed the weakening of presidio life and the escalation of pueblo life. The presidio way of life declined and was eventually deserted in 1835. Seven years later, only one hundred native people remained and lived in the few residual buildings left behind.

Native American conflicts continued as the Mexican government secularized both the missions of San Diego and San Luis Rey in 1834. This resulted in a discord between the native people and the Californios. Rocky economic and political issues ensued, directly affecting the city's population numbers, as they continued to decline. In 1834, San Diego became a pueblo (town) as opposed to a military post, with Juan Maria Osuna as its premiere *alcalde* (mayor). Due to the city's decrease in population its pueblo standing was removed in 1838, and it then became a department of the Los Angeles Pueblo. With the arrival of 1840, San Diego only had roughly 140–150 residents. The presidio slowly slid into decay as San Diego terminated its military town status.

In 1842, Manuel Micheltorena replaced Juan B. Alvarado as the new governor, having been delivered from Mexico to deal with American intrigue into the northwestern prefecture. Americans were already crossing the mountain regions to settle near Sutter's Fort and Sonoma. The Mexican government was fearful of more revolutions and the increasing numbers of Yankee prisoners in their jails. In 1844, California terminated its dependence on Mexico.

American Period (1846–1870)

The US-Mexican War of 1846–48 brought significant changes to San Diego. In 1848, the Treaty of Guadalupe-Hidalgo initiated the commencement of the American Period in San Diego. Thus, the American peoples took total jurisdiction over San Diego. In July 1846, United States armed forces inhabited the City of San Diego. Some people opposed the American side while others happily welcomed it.

Pio Pico's brother, Andres Pico, led a unit of Californios in a battle between United States forces under the command of Gen. Stephen Kearney at the Battle of San Pasqual in December 1846. Many lives were sacrificed as a result of this early morning confrontation. (You will read more about the San Pasqual Battlefield in the pages to come.) In January 1847, two crusades ensued near Los Angeles, resulting in the conquering of the Californios.

Northern California territories expanded rapidly due to the advent of the Gold Rush in 1849. Due to the rising populace it was decided that the region required statehood. Thus, the constitution was written and boundaries were set. In the first election under the American flag the constitution was accepted by California's people. President Fillmore signed the bill on September 7, 1850, with California being admitted to statehood as the thirty-first state of the United States. A few months later, on February 18, San Diego County was officially arranged by the California State Legislature. San Diego's boundaries consisted of Imperial, Riverside, and San Bernardino counties. Just seven months later the city's premiere county elections took place.

In the twenty-five years following 1848, San Diego saw the increase of the Anglo-American community. At the time, the area of Old Town was known as the biggest land development, boasting 48,557 acres of previous pueblos. For the next ten years the city saw limited development. Those living in the city worked on strategies to increase visitors and population growth. They did this by inviting a transcontinental railroad and relocating a new town closer to the bay. This new area was referred to as Graytown or Davis' Folly, in honor of Andrew B. Gray and William Heath Davis.

It was concluded that the bay would serve as the more appropriate site for a seaport. William Heath Davis was one of the men who joined Lt. Andrew B. Gray in developing this new area, which was called New Town. For $2,304, promoters purchased 160 acres and developed the streets. Davis bought cargo consisting of bricks, lumber, and pre-constructed houses that came from the Atlantic coast by way of Cape Horn. Subsequently, a wharf and warehouse were built from the lumber. Eventually, the relocation to New Town from Old Town failed to prosper. Old Town residents then came up with the moniker "Davis' Folly" to describe its declining conditions. (You will hear more about New Town in later chapters.)

Toward the end of the California Gold Rush, New San Diego became abandoned, with only a few lonely structures remaining. At the time of the Civil War and a serious drought, the city became an isolated frontier settlement. In 1850, the population was 650, whereas in 1860, it dropped to a mere 539. It was not until the arrival of land developer Alonzo Horton in 1867, that San Diego prospered into an American municipality.

The true urbanization of San Diego did not officially commence until 1869, when Mr. Horton relocated the center of business and government affairs from Old Town to New Town once again. He had a vision that San Diego would be a modern city and chief seaport. With downtown being closer to the bay it had a direct impact on commercial associations. Basically, Mr. Horton revised Mr. Davis' original plans for New Town.

Sadly, a fire erupted on April 20, 1872, ultimately ruining Old Town's business center. With this event and the 1871 transferral of the county seat to New Town, Old Town's development and administration quickly degenerated. People quickly saw how the availability of public facilities and increased land values positively affected New Town.

Between 1885 and 1890, five independent railroad liners were built due to the city's population increase. San Diego's population rose to 40,000 with the arrival of the transcontinental railroad. This had a positive influence on the building of new edifices and structures. As trading became more prolific building materials became more abundant. Wood started to rapidly replace adobe-constructed sites. In 1890, San Diego's populace decreased significantly due to the United States Depression. Many smaller-run railroad lines went out of business during this time. By 1910, the city had restored itself with the development of new industries and further railroad consolidation. In 1917, only the Santa Fe and John Spreckel's San Diego & Arizona railroad lines operated within the county. Traveling by train thrived in the 1920s, but the automobile rapidly replaced the desire to journey by railway.

Once a portion of Highway 101, Pacific Highway was one of the original roads developed in the city. Highway 101 previously extended down to San Diego and the Mexican border until Interstate 5 replaced it in the 1960s. Overnight automobile camps were popular, as people enjoyed traveling by car to their destinations. Interestingly, by 1904, Southern California was known as a paradise for those who loved to journey via automobile. At the time the route that extended from Los Angeles was described as the most scenic and charming roadway in the nation. By 1907, San Diego's Chamber of Commerce Boulevard Committee set in place concrete plans to build 200 miles. In all, San Diego became a pristine tourist attraction, with Old Town being a hot spot destination that still exists today. In fact, with John Spreckel's desire to initiate the San Diego Electric route through Old Town, it further catered to people's intrigue in Old Town's historical significance. Furthermore, when San Diego hosted the Panama-California Exposition in 1915, Old Town continued to be a viable point of interest for travelers. The flickering of intrigue in restoration and preservation began for the location, which was also referred to as the birthplace of California. (You will hear more about the boomtown days in the paragraphs to come.)

New Town Arrives Again (1870–1889)

New Yorker Alonzo Horton was one of the biggest influencers of New Town. In 1851, he headed west for California, and after many business ventures he settled in San Francisco with his wife, Sarah Wilson Babe. In 1867, Mr. Horton heard about positive opportunities in San Diego. On April 15, 1867, he arrived in California's southernmost city and fell in love with the harbor. He saw Old Town dwindling away, and according to him, the areas near the harbor were the best spots for constructing a new city. He bought 960 acres for $265 and received a deed to the land on May 11. In 1870, the County Board of Supervisors coerced the removal of all county records from the Whaley House in Old Town to the Express Building in New San Diego. The actual removal of records took place in April 1871. In 1872, a fire erupted in Old Town, further hindering its fate. Alas, Old Town seceded.

With the closing of 1870, future economic projections looked positive for San Diego. Real estate was valued at just over $2 million. The population grew to about 3,000 people. Just over 900 occupied residences existed, as well as sixty-nine business sites. The San Diego County Medical Society was initiated in 1870, and had more than seventy physicians and eleven dentists by 1872. In spring 1871, the New Town post office became known as the San Diego post office. A new courthouse was developed on Broadway and Front streets.

In October 1880, the California Southern Railroad was incorporated in the city, with routes starting at National City and traveling through San Diego, Encinitas, and Temeculaand San Jacinto to Colton. On November 9, 1885, the California Southern joined forces with the Atchison, Topeka, and Santa Fe. This directly signaled the "Boom of the Eighties," where passengers could travel from coast to coast in just seven days. Furthermore, provisions such as oranges, lemons, honey, potatoes, fish, salt, butter, and wool could be delivered to new markets. The premiere county fair took place in National City, in September 1880. Fertile crops sprouted in the southeastern portion of San Diego. The boom continued with other business ventures, including the construction of key buildings, such as the Hotel Del Coronado. A gas manufacturing company was developed, as was the San Diego Telephone Company. The Southern California Mountain Water Company was established, providing water to city residents.

The Boomtown Days

When gold was unearthed in Julian in 1870, it had a direct effect on San Diego's port and downtown businesses. Then, in 1872, the "Tom Scott Boom" brought the city's populace up to 4,000 individuals. This occurred when Col. Thomas Scott, president of the Texas & Pacific Railroad, was preparing to lengthen his transcontinental line to the Pacific region. However, it never prospered due to foreign investors' discouragement of the project. Therefore, many people, who so eagerly came into the town, left upon hearing this despondent news.

In 1879, local businessmen joined forces to once again attempt to bring railroad lines to San Diego. Frank Kimball (one of the founders of National City, along with his brother, Warren) traveled to Boston to meet with the president of Santa Fe Company, who had intentions to reach the Pacific in Guaymas, Mexico. Kimball recommended that the railroad extend to the Southern California region. A branch of the Santa Fe system, this railroad finally arrived in 1885. With this a second boom followed, with the city's population increasing to 40,000. The first electric lights and horse cars commenced operation in 1886. The first electric streetcar came about the following year. During this time homes and wharves were constructed, along with various other business edifices. By 1890, the boom had ended, ultimately reducing the populace to a mere 17,000 people.

In the late 1880s and early 1900s, the city's growth was dependent on John D. Spreckels and his brother. They both traveled from San Francisco to San Diego, seeing huge possibilities in the latter. They bought the entire Coronado Beach Company property, which opened the Hotel Del Coronado in February 1888. The brothers' financial investments increased the city's economic self-esteem. Spreckels had a profound impact on San Diego development in the early 1920s.

The Panama-California exposition was perhaps the most historic event in San Diego in the early twentieth century. Celebrating the Panama Canal's opening, San Diego became America's primary port of call. San Diegans envisioned the canal as a means to develop their commercial harbor. It was a substantial undertaking to market and expand the city as an urban hub.

In January 1905, the *San Diego Union* remarked:

> . . . the Canal will mean to San Diego the full development of all her natural resources, agricultural . . . and industrial. It will mean factories, and mills and plants . . . It will mean improvements in that equipment as related to the military and naval development of this part of the Pacific. In short it will bring San Diego into prominence as a city possessing the solid advantages that belong to a great commercial port. The development of the Colorado River Valley in the eastern part of San Diego County . . . is bound to play an important part in the business of the port . . . (*San Diego Union* 1-1-1905)

For the exposition, San Diego organizers sought out 640 acres of city land—later known as Balboa Park—and chose a Spanish Colonial motif as the focal point. When the event took place on January 1, 1915, San Diego was further placed on the map, with two million people showing up in the first year alone. When the exposition closed on January 1, 1917, approximately 3.8 million people came through Balboa Park. As a result Spanish colonial architecture acquired popularity. San Diego leaders also forged relationships, thereby increasing the city's presence as a cultural icon and military town.

San Diego's Contribution to the War Effort

In 1900, San Diego's only connection with the outside world consisted of the Santa Fe's "Surf Line," which ran from Los Angeles. Twenty years later a railroad was eventually constructed through the city's eastern mountains. It was the military that would irreversibly contribute to San Diego's future, as they took advantage of its almost perfect flying weather, beautiful harbor, and tactical significance during national emergencies.

It was San Diego that was named the Southwest site for the War Department's Army division when Congress declared war against Germany in 1917. Camp Kearny was formed, along with Rockwell Field, on Coronado's North Island, commencing the city's future as a Navy town. The US Navy showcased much intrigue in San Diego for naval aviation expansion.

San Diego was an attractive location for aviation pioneers such as Charles Lindbergh, Claude Ryan, B. F. Mahoney, and Reuben Fleet. In fact, Fleet relocated his Consolidated Aircraft Corporation from Buffalo, New York, to San Diego, commencing the foundation of Convair and General Dynamics Corporation. This, in turn, assured the city as a foremost contributor to the US defense industry.

Due to its various naval and Coast Guard facilities, we know that San Diego has long been known as a military city. The Pacific Fleet relocated its headquarters from Honolulu, Hawaii, to the area during the early days of war. As with other locations throughout California, San Diego also endured fears of imminent threats of invasion, so the Army was called in to provide sufficient air defenses.

San Diego was lucky to receive a lot of assistance during the war. The following are just a few of San Diego's war contributions:

> The Amphibious Training Base was situated just south of Coronado, having been obtained by the Navy in summer 1943.
>
> Constructed in 1940, Camp Callan trained coastal artillerymen and antiaircraft gunners. Located three miles north of La Jolla, it stood on what is now the Torrey Pines Golf Course.
>
> Camp Gillespie, now an east county airport, served as a training facility for paratroopers.
>
> Camp Kearney and Camp Elliot eventually became a portion of the Marine Corps Air Station, Miramar, and educated Army infantry and Marine units. As an interesting side note, I currently reside in the community Tierrasanta, which sits atop a portion of Camp Elliot.
>
> In 1942, the Marines attained Camp Joseph H. Pendleton just north of Oceanside. At the time it was the Pacific region's biggest base. With construction commencing in May 1942, its facilities grew at a rapid rate. During the course of World War II various training operations ensued, such as amphibious, ground, air, and auxiliary units. Camp Pendleton's populace grew to include 86,749 individuals in 1944.

> Acquired in 1917, by the US government, San Diego's Naval Air Station, on the northern end of North Island's Silver Strand Peninsula, was utilized as a combined Army and Navy airfield to train World War I pilots. It also served as the Navy's main air station during World War II. In 1955, its name was changed to US Naval Air Station North Island.
>
> The City of San Diego donated terrain to the Navy for the construction of the Naval Training Center, San Diego. Situated at the bay's north end, it trained new recruits by offering them four months of boot camp. When the United States entered the war effort the facility trained 25,000 recruits at one time, in addition to educating personnel on various other subject material.

San Diego's historical timeline consists of various pertinent events that have contributed to it being known as one of the most celebrated cities in the United States. Tourism boomed during the 1920s and 1930s, especially due to the developing movie industry and Tijuana's legal gambling. Furthermore, veterans who were first introduced to San Diego during war times found the city attractive and thus made it their residence. San Diego's economic platform then grew, as many of them secured jobs in the expanding aerospace and defense industry. Even with hardship during the 1960s, "America's Finest City" continued to grow due to real estate interests, increased tourism, and military influence. The 1970s and 1980s, brought ongoing development.

World War II expanded the Navy's affiliation with San Diego, and brought with it a period of accelerated growth up until the end of the Cold War in 1990. San Diego can be credited with bringing a substantial population boom to California, continuing throughout the remaining twentieth century. By 1970, San Diego's populace had increased to 1,357,854 persons. Today the city is still growing, with new businesses, attractions, and residential communities.

PART III:
Central San Diego's Most Haunted

San Diego is known as a historically rich haunted city. In fact, Central San Diego is home to one of the world's most talked about haunted homes, the Whaley House. Other spiritually active sites surround this legendary edifice, attracting history buffs and paranormal researchers alike for many years. One cannot mention the city's ghostly attractions without bringing up the various sites mentioned in this section of the book.

Chapter 3: Calvary Cemetery

In 1873, Joseph Manasse, a Prussian immigrant and shop proprietor, sold a ten-acre plot to the City of San Diego to establish a Protestant and Catholic cemetery. When Father Antonio Ubach, Reverend of the Church of the Immaculate Conception, came around and examined the land, he felt it was too rocky to build a cemetery. Father Ubach had undergone studies to become a priest in Cape Girardeau, Missouri. He then decided to journey to San Diego in 1866, after traveling as a missionary. The terrain was replaced by another lot owned by Manasse in 1876, ultimately becoming Mission Hills Park, a brand new Catholic burial ground. Eventually, Mission Hills Park was founded to serve as a graveyard in place of El Campo Santo in Old Town, San Diego. In 1969, the City of San Diego Historical Site Board elected Calvary Cemetery a historic site.

This new area, situated on a bluff, not only provided extra burial space, but also boasted beautiful views of the bay. Father Ubach approved of this space, laid out the burial spaces, and named it Calvary Cemetery. However, it was never commonly known as Calvary Cemetery, rather referred to as the "New Catholic Cemetery," to differentiate it from the former burial site known as El Campo Santo. In 1988, a memorial of approximately 140 gravestones of historical worth was established and situated in Calvary Pioneer Memorial Park.

Calvary Pioneer Memorial Park is just what is says: a luscious park with various oak trees and other indigenous plants native to the San Diego region. Adjacent to the park is Ulysses S. Grant Elementary School, which commenced services in 1914. When you drive by this beautiful site and see families picnicking and children playing, it is hard to imagine that the physical bodies of once living souls are still interred underneath its confines. Even more inconspicuous are its numerous claims of paranormal activity, which will be discussed.

It is not entirely known how many souls were laid to rest at Calvary Cemetery, but 2007 estimates suggest around 1,650 to as many as 3,400. In fact, more recent research puts the number at 4,000 interred, including many noted San Diego early pioneers. The first burial took place in 1875.

For fifty years Calvary Cemetery catered to San Diego's Catholic community. With the opening of Holy Cross Cemetery in 1919, it eventually fell into disrepair and was then known as the "Old Catholic Cemetery." Sadly, there were signs of neglect and vandals destroying the gravestones. Apparently, the rehabilitation project that took place during the late 1930s and early 1940s, was not enough to salvage the derelict burial grounds.

City leaders such as John (Jack) Stewart, his wife Rosa Machado, and Cave Johnson Couts were buried in Calvary Cemetery. Stewart, who fought in the Battle of San Pasqual, was one of *Two Years Before the Mast* author Richard Henry Dana's shipmates. Cave Johnson Couts was one of the richest men in the entire region, having owned both Rancho Guajome and Rancho Buena Vista Adobe. He was originally buried in El Campo Santo, but was later re-interred in Calvary Cemetery. Father Ubach, known as Las Padre, was also laid to rest here.

The epidemic known as the Spanish Flu (1918–1919) killed more people than World War I. Known as "La Grippe," several million people succumbed to this deadly disease. It comes as no surprise that more individuals were interred at Calvary Cemetery in 1918, than in any other year.

In 1968, the City of San Diego announced the abandonment of Calvary Cemetery, saying it was a health hazard to individuals. Twelve months later, the city had all of the gravestones removed and dumped in a ravine in Mount Hope Cemetery. The public was hugely dissatisfied with this and opted to have the majority of the tombstones buried in a mass grave at Mount Hope.

Getting back to the ghostly claims at this park, the fact that some of the bodies and headstones are in separate places is conjectured why it is one of the most haunted parks in the City of San Diego. Tragically, there seems to be a general spiritual unrest and unhappiness at cemeteries that have had a past of neglect and abandonment.

There are many claims of supernatural activity at this noted park. Apparitional and shadow figure sightings prevail, including disembodied voices and extreme cold spots. There is even a section of the park where many people have captured electronic vocalizations of children. Additionally, there is a general sense of feeling that you are being surveyed by unseen eyes.

I have had many otherworldly experiences while visiting this noted park. I have seen numerous fleeting shadow figures, most likely representing partially manifested apparitions. I have encountered the disembodied footsteps of someone approaching me; however, there is no one around to explain the sounds. Furthermore, I have been touched by invisible hands on the shoulder and back. Occasionally, I have heard faint whispers in my ear and have walked into isolated cold spots.

Many investigators have come into contact with the spirit of a young woman. Some have seen her adorned in a lightly colored dress or gown. She makes appearances underneath a specific tree toward the center of the park. In my opinion, she exhibits intelligent behavior and seems to know when people are trying to communicate with her. To date, we do not know exactly who she is or where she comes from.

There is also a set of gravestones in the far southwestern portion of the park. Many individuals have had ghostly experiences near these markers. Homeless individuals like to nestle in the shrubbery just south of these headstones, possibly explaining some of the documented sightings and sounds.

Chapter 4: Casa De Estudillo

Casa de Estudillo in Old Town San Diego State Historic Park.

One of the most famous adobe homes exists on the southeast side of the plaza in Old Town, San Diego Historic Park. Constructed between 1827–1829 by Lt. Jose Antonio Estudillo, this historic edifice would be the social epicenter of Old Town San Diego during the Mexican and early American era. In 1932, the site was listed on the California Register as Historical Landmark #53. This *casa de poblador* was built as a single-story, L-shaped structure around an inner courtyard. Native American laborers worked around the clock to build this rustic adobe masterpiece, complete with brick-tiled floors, clay-tiled roofs, wood-barred windows, and inner wooden shutters. Some renters resided at the home, which also housed a school during the early 1860s.

Another wing was added to the home in the early 1830s. At that time this adobe castle boasted twelve rooms, consisting of bedrooms, servants' quarters, a kitchen, work and storage rooms, a *sala* (or living room), dining room, and a chapel. Intriguingly, a turreted balcony was placed on the roof so people could observe bullfights, horse races, and plaza parties.

The inner courtyard had several roles. For one, it was the center of entertainment, as well as work. It was the central gathering arena for family fiestas, christenings, and feast day commemorations. Much time was spent among family and friends underneath the verandas. Native American servants cooked bread in beehive-structured ovens, or *hornos*. They also spun cotton, hung clothing items, constructed adobe bricks, groomed horses, and supervised the orchards and gardens.

Mr. Estudillo was born in 1803, in Monterey, and was the sixth child of Jose Maria, Spanish-born *comandante* of the presidio in San Diego. Mr. Estudillo was a well-known man in his day, and during Mexican control he served as town treasurer, tax collector, justice of the peace, and mayor in 1837–1838. In 1850, he reprised these roles during American rule. Furthermore, Jose Antonio also supported the dissolution of the mission system in the early 1830s, and functioned as the *mayordomo* (administrator) of the Mission San Luis Rey from 1840 to 1843. Jose Antonio Estudillo was one of the city's biggest landholders; in 1850, his land properties surpassed $25,000.

In 1824, he wed Maria Victoria Dominguez, daughter of a cavalry sergeant stationed at the presidio. The couple raised their ten children, four grandchildren, and five nieces and nephews in the Estudillo adobe. Furthermore, Victoria also adopted and brought up many Native American orphans in the casa.

Jose Antonio advocated republican self-rule during the time when Mexico struggled for independence from Spain. In 1833, he and five other male citizens came up with a petition encouraging the governor to set in place a civil government instead of ongoing military control by the presidio's *comandante*. Two years later Old Town San Diego became an official pueblo to be managed by a designated town council.

The Estudillo family went through some tenuous times after Jose Antonio passed away on July 19, 1852. In 1855, livestock prices plummeted, and the house was worth a mere $3,500. Additionally, affairs between family and in-laws became progressively strained. For example, during the 1860s, there were about six property transfers and various family member lawsuits.

As time went on the Casa de Estudillo fell into disrepair, especially when it became associated with Helen Hunt Jackson's prized novel *Ramona*. Sadly, visitors came by the masses to visit the home out of the mistaken notion that the chapel was the foundation for the marriage between the book's two main characters, Ramona and Alessandro.

In 1906, the edifice was sold to Nat Titus for a miniscule $500. In 1910, Spreckels leased it to Tommy Getz, a musical performer who hailed from the Midwest region. Getz lacked experience in historic and museum management when he opened the newly restored Casa de Estudillo as a museum and advertised it as "Ramona's Marriage Place" instead of "Casa de Estudillo." In fact, in its June 10 volume, the *Los Angeles Times* proclaimed:

> Old Town is waking! . . . At the very door of one of the oldest adobe houses in the hamlet, which has been entirely restored, as nearly as possible along the old lines, and now hundreds visit Old Town every day where dozens visited it in months in the past. Yes, Old Town is waking and again coming into her own.

In 1910, a wishing well was constructed underneath a pergola at the walkway's finish. Above it was the inscription:

Quaff ye the waters of Ramona's well;

Good luck they bring and secrets tell;

Blest were they be sandaled Friar;

So drink and wish for they desire.

The historic site's grounds were adorned with Native American creations, wagon wheels, and other Spanish-related antiques. Getz gave daily presentations on the region's local history. Intriguingly, many newlyweds were married in the home's candle-lit chapel, which exhibited an extremely old handmade Black Madonna (a statue or painting of the Blessed Virgin Mary). Not surprisingly, the Estudillos probed into the museum's trend under Getz's management. Specifically, they questioned his emphasis on a fabled romance as opposed to the Estudillo family's history. In fact, Jose Guadalupe Estudillo filed a complaint in 1913, suggesting the structure was misnamed. It was later said that the home had appeal due to Helen Hunt Jackson's book, not because it housed the family that bares its name.

The Ramona myth specifically catered to Anglo-American California newcomers, with many of them desiring idyllic values and traditions. These folks came to Southern California when it was in the midst of transforming into a more urbanized, industrialized, and populated area. "Ramona's Marriage Place" was the embodiment of a simpler and more romantic era often linked with the "Days of the Dons." The popularity of Ramona lasted up until the late 1930s.

As the years progressed, the popularity of Ramona gradually faded and the home became known for the family it originally housed. In modern time, Casa de Estudillo is known as a historic Californio adobe home by California State Parks. It was listed on the National Register of Historic Places in 1970, as it represents one of the finest examples in the United States of a standard large Spanish-Mexican one-story residence.

Hazel Wood Waterman was called upon to restore the noted Estudillo mansion. She was mentored by one of San Diego's master architects and possessed a natural grasp of design concepts. She was pulled to restore the home as an archetypal old Spanish California residence, not as it was originally constructed. Additionally, her refurbishing efforts pioneered the utilization of traditional building processes. Today, the Estudillo home is preserved via the traditional use of adobe building methods.

As with other noteworthy historic buildings throughout Old Town, Casa de Estudillo continues to speak of its days past. As you wander around the plaza and stop in front of the renowned landmark you can almost hear the home's voice as it shares its past times with you. As with its neighboring Casa de Bandini/Cosmopolitan

Hotel, the Estudillo residence is known for exuding ghostly energy, mainly residual imprints of years ago.

Many visitors to the house experience spiritual phenomena on a recurring basis. I have talked with staff who have documented seeing apparitions and phantom faces that suddenly appear in mirrors. Some folks have seen the ethereal form of a monk in the former chapel. Others have seen a man dressed in cowboy attire materialize in the dining room. Freezing cold spots appear out of nowhere, along with various light anomalies. Disembodied vocalizations and music playing of its own volition abound at this noted historic residence. Furthermore, there have been occasions where people have heard the slamming shut sound of the heavy wooden doors.

One of my fellow research colleagues told me about the time he witnessed seeing a man looking out of one of the front windows. He went on to say that the ghost's clothing was extremely dated and resembled attire worn in the 1800s. Other people have seen children peeking out of windows, as well.

A few years ago, when I was walking through the Estudillo house, I heard the disembodied sounds of children. There were no children present inside the structure at the time, and the vocalizations strongly sounded as if they were emanating from the site's interior, as opposed to out in the plaza. A few moments after, I noticed that one of the rocking chairs was moving on its own. Could this have been the little girl dressed in Victorian clothing that is often heard or seen inside the building?

As with any location with a haunted reputation, it is important to study the theories behind its ghostly activity. For one, we know that history and the paranormal share a bond; you cannot have one without the other. Of course, it is theorized that paranormal activity can increase as a result of renovations and restoration.

I have speculated whether or not the building's makeshift chapel has added to the mix of paranormal energy. Is it possible that some of the supernatural activity at the adjacent Cosmopolitan Hotel somehow intertwines with the energy at the Estudillo home? Does the legend of Ramona have anything to do with its paranormal energy? What we do know is that the Estudillo clan was a prominent family and its heritage is forever preserved in a home that is dearly loved.

Chapter 5: Cosmopolitan Hotel (Casa De Bandini)

The Cosmopolitan Hotel in Old Town San Diego State Historic Park.

The Cosmopolitan Hotel has an expansive 175-year history, originating with a gentleman by the name of Juan Lorenzo Bandini, a pioneer who settled in the area in the 1800s. Juan was born on October 4, 1800, the son of Capt. Jose Maria Bandini, a Spanish-born naval officer and native of Andalusia. Bandini Jr. went through educational studies in Andalusia and cultivated himself as an admired politician, civic leader, and rancher. Mr. Bandini was a privileged California citizen who saw it transition from Spanish into Mexican control; he took a prominent seat in removing control from the Californians and Americanizing it. Furthermore, he is remembered for his public services in San Diego; as a result, many people considered this man the premiere Spanish citizen of his time period.

Situated in the heart of Old Town, San Diego, Bandini constructed his well-appointed and accommodating home from 1827 to 1829. It boasts a mixture of nineteenth-century Mexican adobe and American wood framing construction practices. The abundantly furnished home featured eight rooms, a *zaguan* kitchen, two patios, and corrals. As the family grew in number more rooms were added to both wings. Water was made available by two man-made wells.

Building of the home was a massive undertaking, utilizing Christianized Native Americans for labor purposes. During the 1830s, adobe houses were scattered about like chess pieces in Old Town. Bandini's thick adobe-walled mansion was the social center of town. In 1846, it even became the headquarters for Commodore Stockton, with Bandini providing needed provisions for his troops.

Bandini's wealth came from cattle ranching, a San Diego business venture appealing to economic success in the 1830s and 1840s. As a well-known figure of Californio culture, Mr. Bandini represented the epitome of magnificent splendor and opulence of his time. He was an educated man well-versed in writing, speaking, and music. He is well-known for offering lavish dance parties (*fandangos*).

Juan Bandini married a woman named Dolores, the daughter of Capt. Jose M. Estudillo. Their three daughters, Josefa, Arcadia, and Ysidora, were known as the most attractive women in all of California. They all resided in Southern California and were well-known, respected citizens. Legend says that it was at this exact mansion that Ysidora fell off the roof into Lt. Cave Johnson Couts' arms while he was positioned on a horse. (You will read more about the Couts family in the Rancho Buena Vista Adobe and Rancho Guajome sections.) Once the United States freed California from Mexico, many Californios struggled with the new American economic system. Juan Lorenzo Bandini thus suffered financially in the 1850s, and was coerced to sell his sprawling estate in 1859, as a way to pay back owed debts. Sadly, his health dramatically declined as well, and later that same year he passed away.

After Bandini's death, American stagecoach operator Albert Seeley planted his eye on Bandini's original structure. He was born in Illinois, and was a stagecoach operator since the age of seventeen. After working in Texas and Los Angeles, Albert and his family decided to relocate to San Diego. Shortly thereafter, he commenced the United States Mail Stage Line. On May 1, 1869, Seeley bought the Bandini residence for $2,000 to provide a depot and accommodations for his line.

He had plans to eventually construct a hotel and stagecoach shop. He envisioned transforming the original residence, making it a place for travelers to revel in comfort and entertainment. The year 1869, marked the debut showcasing of the Cosmopolitan Hotel, where Seeley added a second story to the premises from his wife's $8,000 inheritance. The hotel was an L-shaped Greek Revival structure boasting a billiards room, sitting room, saloon, post office, and barber shop.

In fact, when he converted Bandini's former residence into the newly founded hotel, Old Town was losing its Mexican and Californio temperaments; thus, the historic edifice's new role was a sure cultural change personifying the Frontier lifestyle. Author Victor Walsh relays the following about the newly founded Cosmopolitan Hotel in his article "If Walls Could Speak: San Diego's Historic Casa de Bandini":

> It incorporated new building materials, architectural elements, and interior furnishings and features, as well as such amenities as clocks, newspapers, printed fees, and schedules. It offered a multiplicity of relatively new commercial services, including a post office and barbershop, along with its operation as a hotel, bar, restaurant, and stage

> office. In a word, the hotel embodied what society was becoming: more mobile in terms of distance and speed and more disciplined and exacting in time. It also reflected the differentiation between public and private space that was less sharply delineated in the earlier Mexican era.

In 1869, Albert Seeley constructed Seeley Stables to support transportation services. The horse stables included stalls, wagon storage, and tack rooms on the original floor. Food provisions and straw were lifted to the top floor for storage. In 1888, Seeley sold the Cosmopolitan Hotel, with the stables demolished in 1920. In 1974, the California State Parks reconstructed the property to make way for the Seeley Stable Museum. As railroad lines developed throughout California, Seeley's business gradually declined.

The building's next role served as a functioning canning facility for an olive factory in 1900, converted by Akerman and Tuffley. The two men continued to run the plant until 1919, when they sold their business to a local corporation with San Diego and New York investors. In 1928, Bandini's grandson, Cave J. Couts Jr., obtained ownership of the former building, and in 1930, three succeeding remodeling projects transformed the structure into a lavish tourist destination. The grand structure soon re-emerged as a functioning hotel, complete with a restaurant, wired electricity, gas, and new décor.

James H. and Nora Cardwell then came into the picture in the 1950s, taking proprietorship of the structure, when it became a lavish tourist motel. The year 1968, marked an important time for the building, as the hotel was sold to the State of California and Old Town, and San Diego State Historic Park was initiated.

In October 2010, the San Diego Paranormal Research Society was invited to conduct an overnight ghost research project at the hotel. Prior to our investigation, we ate a delectable meal at Casa Guadalajara, one of the most prized Mexican restaurants in the city. After we finished eating we checked into our hotel rooms at the Cosmopolitan, unpacked our arsenal of equipment, and met to discuss the night's research experiments. We had two natural environmental conditions on our side this particular night: a full moon and potential thunderstorms.

Numerous guests have reported anomalous incidents, especially since the structure's recent remodel reminiscent of the original Cosmopolitan Hotel. At this prized location guests can experience a potpourri of paranormal experiences, including apparitional sightings, feelings of being watched, cold spots, disembodied vocalizations, phantom smells, etc. In fact, the spiritual forms of Juan Lorenzo and Ysidora Bandini, as well as various children, have been witnessed by guests. Theresa Cannizzaro, a local paranormal researcher with Pacific Paranormal Investigations, reported being touched on her arms inside one of the rooms adjacent to the bar. She said that it mimicked a "pins and needles" feeling, which is what many people report after possibly being touched by an unseen entity. Perhaps the building's ethereal residents are just going about their past lives in the present.

Both inclement weather and a full moon phase are theorized to correlate to supernatural activity. The natural ionic energy produced from these conditions can potentially be a capacitor for spiritual energy. Without understanding the exact reasoning for this, full moon nights are hypothesized as helping the manifestation of spiritual energy.

One of the SDPRS members relayed her feelings as she entered the premises:

> As I walked up the steps to the hotel I started to get excited. There is definitely an air of antiquity in the place. I was told by the receptionist that our room was upstairs and in the back. She pointed to the stairs beyond the velvet rope and off I went. I let my gut lead the way and I found our room with ease. The team was there, ready to go and just hanging around until it was time to start our investigation. We had to wait for the dinner guests to finish their meals.

One of the problems we ran into was the loud noise emanating from the hotel's outside bar area, so we decided to wait until after the bar closed to proceed with our investigation. By that time it was well after 1:00 a.m. and some of the team members were experiencing fatigue. Regardless of the circumstances, we prevailed and were able to devote about six hours to our research project.

We stayed in room 11 at the Cosmopolitan Hotel, and several of us started to immediately sense its historical past. When I first entered Room 11 I was immediately struck by a vertigo sensation, and I intuitively sensed two female energies. At one point I thought I heard shuffling in the bathroom. A sound also came from my red bag, which was on the floor, as if someone was rustling through it.

We had a local medium attend our investigation of the Cosmopolitan Hotel. Upon his immediate entrance to room 11, he too was met with historical vibrations of the past. Corroborating my experience, he commenced communication with a female he called the "Lady of the House." He further validated another member's mental image of the older man, saying that his name was Williams or Watson. One member relayed:

> . . . almost immediately after being in the room I began to get an image of an older man. He was a working man, balding and weathered. His clothes were dirty, slightly tattered, and quite old. He liked to drink and staggered a bit. I thought I heard his low-calling voice a couple times, but I could not be certain it was him. However, for the next hour or so I continued to receive his images. I looked around the room a bit and also out the windows.

According to our guest medium, he felt that this elderly soul was a barn hand who was attracted to the bottle (alcoholic). He also sensed that this male presence started a small fire in the barn. Additionally, our intuitive guest had the strong sense that Mrs. Seeley was not satisfied with the building's remodel.

The entire team split up into two separate groups of three people covering several different rooms inside the Cosmopolitan Hotel. The areas we investigated included paranormal hot spot locations, such as the wine room, main dining hall, and upstairs private guest rooms. Indeed, the entire experience proved to be fascinating and eye-opening.

I captured several contextually significant EVP responses to my questions in the main dining hall. Since the Cosmopolitan Hotel was known for throwing lavish parties I made sure to acknowledge that in my questions. After asking, "Did you have parties in here?" a female vocalization came through seconds after. Additionally, after asking who constructed the entire building, we received an anomalous response, "Albert," indicating a historically relevant vocalization. Was this energy referring to Albert Seeley?

Throughout our time spent in the main dining hall several SDPRS members reported feeling as though they were being watched. One of our former members felt some unseen presence touch her shoulder. She immediately began to adjust her body as a way to rule out accidentally brushing up against a curtain or touching one of the tables. Furthermore, she told us that the touch felt oddly cold and gave her a prickly sensation. Our Los Angeles area representative heard footsteps and shuffling; an odd occurrence in the room, since all investigators were stationary at the time.

About twenty minutes into our audio experimentation, I started to sense an ethereal presence of a small child. What is intriguing—as I kept my impression to myself—was how two members visually saw a humanoid shadow form just moments after I had my intuitive feeling. Feeling as though the spiritual energy of a boy was among us, I made a point of asking him to speak to us. Shortly after asking what his name was I received a male EVP saying, "Stefan."

Our Los Angeles area representative further echoes the experiences we had while researching the main dining room. In her own words:

> I was teamed with Nicole and Joy. During the initial walkthrough I had my audio recorder and digital camera on hand. As a group, we experimented with Nicole's Laser Grid and the Ghost Box in the dining room and bar. We also worked with Delia's dowsing rods and an EMF detector.
>
> We began the first EVP session in the dining room at about 11:15 p.m. and ended about 11:45 p.m. Personal experiences included Joy being touched on the shoulder and odd sounds emanating from the small tearoom behind us. Nicole mentioned sensing a change of energy in the room during the session and the ethereal presence standing in the area behind Joy. I also noticed something behind her for a moment, but since there was a reflection of light from a streetlight, I could not be sure that what I saw was paranormal.
>
> We all heard a strange whistling from outside which shows up on my

> EVP recording. Other sounds that were caught on my recorder included faint, almost constant piano music during the first half of the session, including a louder version directly after Nicole asked for the spirit to play the piano. At 9:15 recorder time a harp strum can be heard.

Perhaps one of the most intriguing and spine-tingling experiences of the night occurred in the former Bandini kitchen, known as the wine room. Delia conducted some electromagnetic field and baseline temperature tests prior to us conducting Instrumental Trans Communication work (real-time audio work with spiritual energy). According to our environmental meters, the EMF levels were 0 mg and the temperature was an even 70.1°F.

Once we gathered around a table and started asking questions, the energy changed from a stagnant emptiness to a fully crowded room. At one point the temperature dropped three degrees, only to return to its original reading a few moments later. Delia experimented with her divining rods with significant results. At this time we felt it was appropriate to conduct our ITC session utilizing an old Radio Shack® hack device. At one point we received a real-time response, "House," when asking about the structure. Additionally, when we inquired as to what spiritual presence was with us, we received a real-time female response, "Ysidora," as in possibly Ysidora Bandini. We also heard the word "cocina" come through, which is Spanish for "kitchen." Furthermore, Delia asked for any intelligent ethereal energies to "stop the radio from scanning." Since this was a pure experiment, we were delighted when our ITC device seemingly discontinued its scanning, as it really cannot do so without a human pressing down on the button.

With only a few minutes into our session we were met with a hair-raising experience—to date, it is one of the most profound audio captures ever in the history of SDPRS. Furthermore, this event in time most likely correlates to the Native American history prevalent in San Diego County. You see, after asking a series of questions our ITC device mysteriously stopped scanning on Native American chanting. Yes, that is correct: Native American chanting. Is it possible that our device stopped on a local radio station that happened to be broadcasting this musical mantra? I guess it is always possible.

On closer inspection, our device not only discontinued its scanning of AM radio bands, but it also stopped at the exact beginning of this Native American hymn. It is this fact, coupled with San Diego native peoples' history, that caused us to deem this experience something quite supernatural. Apparently Ramona married her husband at Casa de Bandini. Her ethnicity was part Hispanic and Native American. Casa de Estudillo is directly across from the hotel, which has another strong Native American connection. Was the spiritual energy of the Native Americans speaking to us via this event? Did they have a message for us? Next time we conduct further research at the Cosmopolitan Hotel we will delve more into the meaning of this phenomenon.

After spending a considerable amount of time inside the wine room, we decided to investigate the parlor area, another hot spot for paranormal activity at the Cosmopolitan Hotel. All of us documented hearing loud footsteps directly above us. Most of the rooms were empty that night and many of the employees had already left for the evening, so we could not account for the noise. We were then prompted to head upstairs to inquire about the footsteps. We attempted to rule out living souls moving upstairs, but were met with complete silence; thus, we could not determine the origin of the stomping noises from directly upstairs. It must be said that there are numerous claims of guests hearing disembodied foot movements inside the hotel rooms.

About eight minutes into our parlor investigation experimentation we documented hearing the disembodied sounds of laughing children. There were no children inside the building at that time, nor were there any youths outside. The potentially anomalous sounds were emanating from the tea room. These seemingly ethereal children prompted me to ask questions. Therefore, I asked the children how they were feeling, only to be met with a ghostly EVP of a small child saying, "happy." This response seemed to directly correlate to the incorporeal laughter we heard moments prior.

As with many other Old Town, San Diego, noted locations, the Cosmopolitan Hotel is indeed a historical gem. The people of its past seem to continue their vibrations and share their legacy with visitors from all walks of life. The hotel seems to include a mixture of residual and intelligent ethereal energy, all of which help to paint an overall picture of its days past—a past that continues to shine among current time periods. When you visit the Cosmopolitan, make sure to say hello and thank the people responsible for this structure's success.

Chapter 6: El Campo Santo Cemetery

El Campo Santo Cemetery in Old Town, San Diego, State Historic Park

In 1837, Father Narciso Duran, a Franciscan friar and missionary, approached the pueblo council about reserving land for a community burial site. A small and quaint cemetery sits in the heart of Old Town, San Diego. Known as El Campo Santo Cemetery, this quiet setting is the eternal resting place of many well-known early San Diego pioneers. The second oldest graveyard in San Diego, El Campo Santo dates to 1849, with the burial of Juan Adams. Old Town residents were originally buried at the Presidio until Juan Adams was laid to rest at El Campo Santo. In fact, the last known burials in the Presidio chapel occurred in the early days of 1849, including the internment of Henry Delano Fitch (1827 baptismal name Enrique Domingo) and a daughter. The burial of people continued through 1880, with many San Diego residents from all walks of life. In fact, more than 500 people were buried in this small location known as the "Holy Field."

In 1889, San Diego Avenue was constructed, a horse-drawn streetcar line built right through portions of the cemetery. In the late 1920s, the church deserted El Campo Santo. In 1942, the line was paved, ultimately leaving seventeen resting spots under the street and sidewalk and thirteen plots under Linwood Street. Sadly, this resting place was neglected over time and deteriorated throughout the years. The San Diego Historical Society came to its rescue in 1933, and dedicated itself to restoring the cemetery as precisely as possible. As part of the restoration an adobe wall was constructed, as well as reset markers, renovated fence enclosures, and a white cross situated in each plot's center.

A plaque exists at the entrance of the burial ground saying, "The restoration of this historic cemetery is the result of the loving and unselfish efforts of Lawrence D. Riveroll as a gift to the people of Old Town." As the Holy Field's curator, Mr. Riveroll worked diligently to secure government funding to construct paling fences and characteristic ornamental borders to serve as grave marker protection from wildlife.

As with many historical locations within Old Town, San Diego, El Campo Santo Cemetery is known for its paranormal phenomena. Many people have experienced incorporeal activity while visiting the confines of the cemetery. I do not believe in conducting paranormal research at cemeteries, as I feel it may disturb the final rest of those interred. However, I have personally visited this necropolis on many occasions, having encountered otherworldly events that defy logical explanation.

One of the prevailing theories as to why supernatural energy emanates from this Catholic burial ground has to do with its years of abuse and neglect. In 1989, Riveroll found the small burial site in sad condition, the majority of it consisting of dirt and small patches of grass. Despondently, he only saw six marked grave sites. As someone who cared strongly about San Diego history, he started to put up stones and markers for the people buried there. According to *San Diego Union Tribune* staff writer John Wilkens, the cemetery walls were moved sixty years ago, causing them to be pinched in approximately twelve feet and some graves to be left behind. As previously mentioned, the markers were able to be found again.

In 1931, the state legislature developed the program of state numbering and registration of historically relevant sites in California. These locations were supplied numbers in the order in which their applications were approved by the state. El Campo Santo, also known as the "Old Spanish Cemetery," was given number 68 on December 6, 1932.

Some people have postulated that the spiritual energies are dissatisfied with how the land they were laid to rest in has suffered over the years. As a paranormal researcher and investigator, I have seen a pattern develop with the mistreatment of historical locations: There seems to be a strong correlation between notable locations in derelict condition and paranormal activity.

Tales abound of restless ethereal energies wandering throughout the graves. Intriguingly, vehicles parked in front of the cemetery may have intermittent trouble starting their engines, as well as car alarms mysteriously setting off for no apparent reason. Furthermore, adjacent commercial businesses have complained of electric problems. Visitors have reported seeing apparitions with Native American and Hispanic ethnicities.

Ghostly shadow humanoid figures have been seen floating throughout El Campo Santo. Are these figures residual energies of the land? Are they partially manifested apparitions of early San Diego citizens? It is hard to tell; however, one aspect remains universally consistent: these figures, as well as more solid specters, all tell a story of this cemetery's known haunted fables.

Many visitors have documented hearing disembodied whispers in their ear when no one else is around. On warm days and nights people will directly walk into an extreme cold spot which seemingly vanishes just moments later. At times, you will feel as though many unseen eyes are watching your every move.

El Campo Santo Cemetery is indeed a special place in San Diego. Many of the people laid to rest there were considered early-day pioneers who helped found "America's Finest City." Those interred came from a melting pot of cultures and nationalities, including German, Irish, Italian, English, and Mexican. Today, the cemetery has more than fifty symbolic markers and crosses—a testament to the souls who are eternally remembered for their contributions to San Diego's noted history.

In all, 477 adults and children were laid to rest in and out of the confines of El Campo Santo.

Chapter 7: El Fandango Restaurant

The abandoned remains of the El Fandango restaurant.

The now permanently closed El Fandango restaurant was actually the home of the Machado family. Jose Manuel Machado was one of the premiere soldiers stationed at San Diego's Presidio, as well as one of the first pioneers of Old Town. Born in 1756, he arrived in the San Diego area in 1781. It is not exactly known where Mr. Machado came from. At fifty-three years of age he wed a young woman named Maria Serafina de la Luz. It has been speculated that their wedding took place about a year before the birth of their first child, Juan, in 1809. Her birth date is recorded as September 1, 1788, which can be found at Our Lady of Sorrows Rectory in Santa Barbara, California.

During that time and for about twenty years after, Jose and his budding family resided within the confines of the San Diego Presidio. When members of the military married their significant others and commenced raising families, living conditions within the presidio progressively declined. Houses soon developed below the hill, especially when imminent attacks by natives lessened. The first of these structures was built in 1820, and Jose Machado was considered one of these early builders. He subsequently selected a plot just southwest of the Capt. Francisco Maria Ruiz dwelling and assembled a one-story adobe in approximately 1830. The eventual Machado home address was 2724 Congress Street after house numbering and streets were developed. The arranged marriage between Jose and Maria produced five boys and five girls. These children became valued citizens of San Diego.

During the early 1830s, brisk trade developed between New England and California, and many vessels visited and remained at ports in San Diego, Santa Barbara, Monterey, and San Francisco. Pilot John Collins Stewart came to San Diego on one of these liners. Known as El Pilato, he worked with the volunteer troops in San Diego during the 1851 Garra Indian uprising. He wed Rosa Machado, the two marrying in February 1845. After John and Rosa tied the knot, the two moved into the latter's parents' home. The two families shared this home during Jose and Maria's remaining years. John and Rosa had eleven children and many grandchildren and great-grandchildren. After the passing of Rosa's parents, the Stewarts remained in the Machado house for the entire length of their married lives.

In 1838, this structure was sold to Juan Machado, one of three mansions the family owned. It was known as Calle de Panaderia de Juan Machado once the edifice was fully constructed. In 1843, the property was expanded and later subdivided, then sold to incoming Americans for business reasons. Many other businesses were established over the years on the site of this historic structure. In 1857, the building was partially leased to Walter Ringgold and Thomas Whaley for commercial purposes, including the Columbia Billard Saloon, a bakery, and another family residence.

In 1858, this particular Machado house burned to the ground and was completely desecrated. The El Fandango restaurant was built atop these ruins. The name referring to the lavish parties known as *fandangos*, the upstairs portions of the building were reserved for banquets and office spaces, whereas the downstairs boasted a nice dining room and outside veranda. The menu offered a variety of select Mexican fare, along with other various cuisines developed in San Diego when people of all walks of life traveled to the area during the Gold Rush days.

Along with many locations in Old Town, Casa de Machado is known for its paranormal activity through the years. There have not been a lot of ghost research projects at the site; however, that has no bearing on the spiritual inhabitants residing at the home. There was an investigation conducted in 1992, according to researcher Dennis William Hauk.

The most prevailing account of ethereal energy at the site is that of a female apparition known as the "Lady in White." A local newspaper article was written in honor of this entity in 1987. She is often seen as a white, wispy, ghostly form in Victorian clothing who sits at tables, moves around the restaurant, and into its walls. Most likely a residual form of psychic energy, this matriarchal spirit form seems unaware of her environment and those living in the mortal realm.

Since she has a distressing disposition, many people associate her presence with that of La Llorona, a legendary ghost prominent in Mexico's folklore. According to the myth, this ghost is often heard weeping near the river as she is looking for her lost children. Others postulate that she is the ghost of Señora Maria Antonia Machado de Silva, who ran to Old Town's center plaza and rescued the Mexican flag while United States armed forces seized San Diego in 1846. No one knows exactly who she is; many speculate that she is a Machado family member who tragically perished in the 1858 fire.

In June 2016, I walked by this vacant site, its walls feeling the empty void and longing for the days of its past. As I was intently looking through the windows and into its bare rooms, I intuitively felt that the energies of this historic edifice are concerned about its emptiness, unquestionably yearning for the livelihood of its former days. I strongly sensed a female presence that echoed these aforementioned sentiments. Perhaps I came into contact with the location's matriarchal spirit known as the Lady in White.

Is it possible that some of the paranormal activity from the neighboring Casa de Estudillo and Cosmopolitan Hotel make their way to the former Machado home? Quite possibly, yes. Since many of these historic families of Old Town knew each other in the mortal realm, perhaps they continue to visit each other in the spiritual realm.

Chapter 8: Serra Museum and Presidio Hill

The Junípero Serra Museum proudly sits on top of Presidio Hill.

As the birthplace of California, the Presidio of San Diego was established in 1769, by the first Europeans to forever live in the state. In the 1920s, it was an empty area of wild oats, cactus, and other shrubs enclosing the original Spanish presidio's decrepit walls. The original Mission San Diego de Alcalá, founded by Father Junípero Serra on July 16, 1769, was formally west of the parking lot below the museum. Due to the hostilities between the Native Americans and soldiers a newer mission was established in 1774, in Mission Valley.

Originally from Mallorca, in the Balearic Islands, Father Serra—a Franciscan monk—envisioned the development of a series of missions to help colonize "New" California. Along with Don Gaspar de Portolá, Father Serra traveled from Baja, California, to dedicate all of the twenty-one missions built throughout the Golden State. Unfortunately, in 1783, Serra passed away in Carmel, and was unable to visualize the finishing of his enormous task. When he arrived at the presidio he planted a cross, said mass, and dedicated the grounds and its original mission to San Diego de Alcalá.

We have to give much thanks to George W. Marston, San Diego's leading merchant and philanthropist at the time, as he helped this location (Old Town) become the birthplace of California. By 1927, Mr. Marston had obtained twenty acres and is responsible for having it and its adjoining fifteen acres dedicated to the presidio's park. The actual construction of the museum came after, representing Spanish mission architecture. It was formally dedicated July 16, 1929, on the 160th anniversary of San Diego. Marston strongly believed in preservation of the site as a way to memorialize Father Serra. It also became home to the San Diego History Center. In a letter to city officials Marston exclaimed:

> The builders of Presidio Park have sought to preserve its inherent forms and to enhance this physical character with deeper meaning and significance . . . Presidio is a symbol of the great years of the discovery by Europeans of a new world. It is evident to any thoughtful person that the integrity of this great landmark, as now almost completely landscaped and improved, should be maintained.

On the 160th anniversary of San Diego, the thirty-seven acres of Presidio Hill was presented to the city by George W. Marston and is at the intersection of Twiggs Street and Cosoy Way. In July 1937, it was officially accepted. John Nolen was responsible for the landscaping, with P. C. Broell continuing on the work since 1932. Remnants of the Spanish occupation still exist within the park, consisting of portions of houses and walls, a brass cannon, and a museum filled with artifacts from its originating days.

A decent-sized Kumeyaay Native American village of approximately 300 people was established on Presidio Hill. Before the arrival of the Spanish peoples in 1769, village occupants lived in woven-grass homes called tules. These native individuals were adept at land management skills, also utilizing the nearby foothills, rivers, and

Disembodied vocalizations are heard, apparitional sightings are seen, and cold spots are felt inside the Junípero Serra Museum.

canyons for their survival. This, coupled with the attractive San Diego climate, made life quite sustainable for these early tribes.

An interpretation of Father Junípero Serra on July 3, 1769, reads as follows:

> . . . We have seen the Indians in immense numbers; and all those on this coast of the Pacific contrive to make a good subsistence on various seeds and by fishing; this they carry on bemeans of rafts or canoes made of tule in which they go a great way to sea. They are very civil. All the males, old and young, go naked; the women; however, and even the female children, were decently covered from their breasts downward. We found in our journey as well as in the places where we stopped, that they treated us with as much confidence and good will as if they had known us all their lives, but when we offered them any of our victuals [provisions] they always refused them. All they cared for was cloth, and for this they would exchange their fish or whatever they had.
>
> From this port and intended mission of San Diego, in Northern California, July 3rd, 1769. I kiss the hands of your Reverence, and am your affectionate brother and servant.
>
> –Fr. Junípero Serra

On September 28, 1542, the Native Americans made their first contact with European explorers when Juan Rodriguez Cabrillo sailed into San Diego Bay and lowered his anchor at Point Loma. As time went on, when Spanish settlements sprouted in Baja and Alta, California, the native peoples' way of life was about to change dramatically. For one, they were converted to Catholicism, which did not sit too well with them, and as a result violence ensued. One historian noted:

> Violence was a constant element of this [Spanish] society from the conquest forward. Subordination of the native people in Southern California was accomplished quickly, as previous visits by foreigners created epidemics of European diseases that reduced and weakened native populations and their ability to rebel.

The presidio's view of the bay was instrumental for the Spanish, as it helped them to monitor potential arriving invaders. Sadly, it was also a symbol of their control over the Kumeyaay people, as they forced the natives into arduous labor. Spanish soldiers guarded the mission with the utilization of livestock and crops, and limited any trading with foreign countries as a way to decrease extraneous influence on the current inhabitants. In 1773 and 1774, wooden structures replaced the original huts built by the Native Americans. As the center of Spanish colonization, strategic Presidio Hill served as San Diego's civil and political center.

In 1938, a tiny fort was constructed by the Mexican townspeople as a means of defense against a Native American uprising. The poorly secured fort on the presidio enclosed a barracks, officers' quarters, a commanding officer's home, servants' areas, a medical facility, chapel, guard house, storehouse, a corral, and some other dwellings. It was a time when Native Americans were holding off on an attack on the soldiers. Even marriages occurred between Native American women and soldiers. Commander Samuel Dupont occupied its space when he arrived with American forces in 1846. When Commander Robert Stockton arrived and made further renovations to the fort a few months later, it was then named in honor of him.

It was not until 1800, when the first American ship, *Betsy*, arrived in San Diego Bay. A couple years later, two other ships arrived with the intention of smuggling otter skins out of San Diego. For sure, this marked the beginning of foreign trade activities along the California coast. Mexico encouraged these foreign trading practices along the state's coast, with San Diego becoming an optimum location for hide trading.

After the secularization of missions by the Mexican government in 1833, the Kumeyaay tribes were sadly exploited by affluent Mexican rancheros. The Spanish surrendered the presidio on April 20, 1822. This commenced the beginning of the Spanish rancho lifestyle, where the wealthy ultimately controlled the former mission lands and those inhabited by the Native Americans. When 1846 came along, the Spanish no longer had control of the area and the Americans took over. In fact, the Americans used Presidio Hill during the Mexican-American War with Commodore Robert Stockton's arrival and establishment of a garrison to house soldiers.

The land at the base of Presidio Hill, known as Old Town, San Diego, lies below where presidio soldiers established home sites. Capt. Francisco Maria Ruiz is remembered for constructing the first adobe house there in 1820. As time went on and more soldiers and settlers traveled from Mexico the colony grew into a town. By the time 1829 hit, approximately thirty homes existed. Furthermore, it had one of the biggest revenues due to its prolific hide trading.

The iconic Serra Museum is reminiscent of Spanish Mission architecture, with white stucco walls, a red-tiled roof, and deeply set windows. Currently the San Diego History Center operates the museum, known for its anthropological collections of historical intrigue. Splendid views await you as you stand outside the structure. To the west, you can see San Diego Bay and other scenic sites. As you travel north, you are presented with a splendid view of Mission Valley. If you look in a southward direction, you can see San Diego International Airport and parts of downtown San Diego. As you walk inside the extraordinary museum you are immediately placed back in time.

There are other important historical items situated outside on the museum grounds. Author Bill Virden, in the 1962 edition of the *San Diego Historical Society Quarterly*, discusses them:

> Walking downhill at the bend of the road to the right is the "Presidio Wall," which was recreated approximately on the location of the easterly limit of the Presidio; a series of lawn-covered mounds, in straight

Presidio Hill is one of the most picturesque settings in San Diego.

> easterly-westerly lines, are all that is left of the crumbled adobe ruins of the original buildings. One room, at the far northwest corner on a bluff overlooking Mission Valley, was left uncovered, and here one may see the original tile floor of this Spanish building nearly two centuries old. While in this area note the large bronze Indian statue, the work of a noted sculptor, the late Arthur Putnam. Cross the road onto the lawn and observe the famous Serra Cross, built in 1913 by the Order of Panama, and faced with broken fragments of the original Spanish tiles. Climb to the cross which has behind it, in a sunken, tree-shaded vale, the equally famous bronze statue of Father Serra, also by Putnam. This statue has always been a delight to amateur photographers. Going up the hill, to the south, at the top of which is the highest point of land in the park, surrounding the flagpole, will be found the open trenches, now landscaped, which were Fort Stockton. Nearby is a commemorative marker to the Mormon Battallion, whose overland journey from Council Bluffs, Iowa, to San Diego is still the longest infantry march in history. Near the flagpole is the old bronze cannon El Jupiter, cast in Manila in the eighteenth century, and once a part of the Spanish defenses of San Diego.

In 2012, the San Diego Historical Society invited the San Diego Paranormal Research Society to host a couple public fundraising tours at the Serra Museum. Similar to its "Spirits of the Adobe" tours at Rancho Buena Vista Adobe, they concentrated on both history and the paranormal. Gabe Selak, the center's former programs manager (Gabe is now the current history ambassador to the San Diego History Center) and historical consultant to the SDPRS, was on hand to talk with guests about the Serra Museum and presidio's past. In addition to the tours, the SDPRS team has also conducted two private research projects inside the museum.

Again, with all of the historical layers, it is not that surprising that both the presidio and Serra Museum have paranormal activity. There are various claims of anomalous phenomena that occur at the two locations. Residual energy remains in historically rich locations, including the various emotions and feelings imprinted on the land. Many people, including myself, have had feelings of sadness, despair, fear, and anxiety while driving up the hill to the presidio. I feel that this directly correlates to the site's Native American and Spanish periods. However, a general sense of peace exists once you step inside the picturesque museum.

Furthermore, many visitors have reported ghostly figures and humanoid shadow forms darting about the area. Some even claim to have spotted Father Junípero Serra roaming the grounds. (I will talk more about my possible experiences with Serra's spirit in a bit.) One of the most fascinating paranormal accounts has to do with a white phantom deer that is occasionally seen in the bushes; several people have described seeing it manifest and disappear right before their eyes.

Even though they are not considered tangible evidence, personal impressions and/or encounters with spiritual phenomena are just as important in telling the overall story of a location's ghostly inhabitants. At least, this is my opinion. I have had various intuitive impressions while visiting and investigating the presidio and Serra Museum.

In 2013, during a private investigation, we had an intriguing experience while conducting a dowsing rod experiment at the iconic location. When I asked Father Serra if he was present at the facility the rods crossed immediately, indicating an answer, "yes." Prior to the investigation, my mom and I decided to walk around, as it was a beautiful dusk evening. At one point my legs felt quite weak. I immediately thought of Father Serra and how he suffered from horrific pain in his legs as he walked miles to his destinations in California.

Furthermore, while we were conducting an EVP and ITC session with the Ovilus X device, we specifically directed our questions to Father Serra. At one point the word "priest" came through the ITC device. I then asked him if he was still present with us in the room, and I heard an audible response, "sí." We also asked him about all of the languages he was known to speak, and a few moments later the word "German" came through the Ovilus X. In his spirit form some people feel that Father Serra is a mean individual. To be honest, I do not get that feeling about him at all. My research has led me to believe that he is ethereally watching over the museum aptly named after him. In my opinion, his energy is gentle and kind.

During the night we also communicated with a woman and her daughter with Native American heritage. In fact, the parking lot to the west of the museum used to be the site of a Native American village. Throughout the night I audibly heard the vocalizations of women and children. At one point during the investigation a team member noticed an anomalous figure moving around the replicated hut inside the main room of the museum.

My mom, Norma Strickland, attended the night's research project. In her own

Vibrations from the past are felt by touching the historic wine press outside the museum.

words she describes a unique experience she had:

> While sitting on the floor in the exhibit room of the Serra Museum, with the lights down low and in a circle with the other members of the group, I observed the area of rug pulsating under the Ovilus device. It had an appearance of life—living breath—which I believe I verbalized to the group. I continued to be drawn to this motion and remember feeling sensations of warmth and cold. This lasted for several minutes.

My mom's experience was quite fascinating, as the Ovilus X repeated the word "light" three times and "under light" one time. Many researchers feel that the Ovilus device is subjective; however, when it reiterates the same words, it could be more indicative of intelligent communication. In the following paragraph you will see how both the ITC device and my audio recorder seemed to work in unison, pointing to a corroboration of events. When this happens I consider it golden data, as two pieces of a puzzle connect.

After these interesting words I asked the question, "Can you be more specific of what light you are under? Are you under the blue light on the floor [referring to the blue light emanating from my device's speaker] or the light from the windows?" Upon review of my audio, I nearly gasped when I heard an EVP response, "under the light." Even more spine-tingling was how the Ovilus spewed out the word "light" for the fourth time. This occurred right at the exact time of the above mentioned EVP! Did my mom's experience correlate to these series of events? Is it coincidental that she noticed pulsating movements underneath that area of the rug at the same time? There is no proof either way, but I strongly feel that Norma's encounter directly

Inside the Serra Museum.

relates to what occurred. You are approaching the Holy Grail when you have a personal experience possibly supported by scientific data.

During one of the SDPRS's fundraising tours the group had a captivating experience in front of the wine press outside the main entrance doors to the museum. The second we approached it Gabe and I were engulfed with an extreme sense of sadness, so much so that I almost shed some tears. By utilizing psychometry, I put my hand on the press to see if I could acquire any more impressions that may still be imprinted on it from years ago. I immediately had a powerful inclination that someone suffered an accidental death while working with the device. This feeling was so strong that I had to lift my hand away from the press.

Many of the guests placed their hands on the antique item after I finished discussing the psychometry method commonly employed during paranormal research investigations. Almost immediately several guests started to feel the wine press vibrate of its own volition. Some people even felt the device move. The unit is very heavy, and even with all of our weight combined it was still not enough to move it.

Gabe and I are continuing our research to see if there are any documented deaths that occurred while operating the ancient apparatus. When you visit this celebrated site take some time to visit the aged wine press, as it seemingly shares the story of its past days.

This is just a thought, but I wonder if my mom's sighting of the pulsating rug is similar to what we were feeling with the press. Is it possible that the energy was similar, the only difference being sight versus touch? Is it possible that the Serra Museum is sharing its past through these present-day vibrations? History infiltrates all areas of the museum and its adjacent grounds.

An archeological program began in 1965, on the presidio grounds and lasted through 1997. By examining the Serra Museum and its adjacent land we can learn a lot about the various groups that inhabited the area. By looking at their similarities and differences we can get a good perception of their visions and viewpoints, all of which contributed to the overall story of this iconic hill overlooking San Diego Bay. Today, a new chapter begins as we study the people of its past and those that play a pivotal role in its present. For sure, in helping to shape the City of San Diego, both the presidio and its historical museum provide visitors from all walks of life the chance to learn about its civic, cultural, and environmental influences.

Chapter 9:
The Whaley House

Known as America's most haunted house, the Whaley House is on San Diego Avenue in Old Town State Historic Park.

> I have a fine lot 150 × 217 1/2 which I shall enclose with a wall sometime this year. I am now building a grainary of brick which will hold 3 or 400,000 pounds of grain. I shall put up sheds for hay, a house and a store of brick. I have over 150 thousand bricks left after putting up my grainary, and if I don't dispose of them soon I shall convert them all into houses and rent them. I have plenty of my own land to build upon. I have a fine rockaway carriage and a span of sorrels, with harness of silver . . . The carriage holds four or six persons . . . My wife has every comfort and luxury I can afford to give her, and we enjoy ourselves to the envy of many. My parlor is furnished with Brussels carpet and mahogany and rosewood furniture, a mahogany crib for little Frank. We frequently have musical soirees and our house is the resort of most of the best people in the place. My wife is the best little woman in the world, loved by all, she is proficient in music, plays and sings.
> –Thomas Whaley

Listed as both a California and National Historical Landmark, the Whaley House is one of the most historical, iconic structures ever built in San Diego. Indeed, this edifice, as well as the family who resided within its walls, has experienced more chronological events than any other residence or family in the city. Thomas Whaley commenced construction of his celebrated home in 1856, which became the first modern two-story Greek revival building in San Diego. The brick used to assemble the well-known home came from Mr. Whaley's own brickyard and was made from river sand and clay. Its woodwork traveled around Cape Horn.

He even exclaimed, "My new house, when completed, will be the handsomest, most comfortable and convenient place in town or within 150 miles of here." The visionary Thomas Whaley even utilized popular New York building plans of the time when erecting his home. In her San Diego Historical Society article about the home, author June Strudwick remarked, "The formal spacings of the doors, windows, heavy porch posts; the nicely cut moldings, the contrast of white detail and red brick, the concealed roof, and essential simplicity are all typical of the Greek Revival that flourished in the United States from 1820 to 1860."

The exquisite home held some of the finest items of the day, including rosewood and mahogany furniture, Brussels carpets, and damask drapes. For sure, this mansion in its day was the talk of the town. The upper floors were reserved for the family's living quarters, whereas the first floor housed the general store. The Save Our Heritage Organization (SOHO) took over management of the home in 2000, and has diligently worked to clean and restore the site after years of neglect and abandonment.

Having one of the most colored histories in the entire United States, the Whaley House has taken on several roles in its lifetime. A well-appointed home for the family of its namesake, the building also served as a granary, San Diego's first commercial theater, and various businesses, such as Mr. Whaley's general store and the county courthouse. Furthermore, it has endured and survived its share of tragedies, including fires, earthquakes, and vandalism. History serves as a blueprint for spiritual phenomena; one can imagine the paranormal activity that exists due to the countless stories evolving around this building, a structure that very well serves as an embodiment of San Diego history. In fact, United States Commerce has endorsed the hauntings that take place at this California Landmark.

Thomas Whaley built his home for a mere $10,000, completing in 1857. A man with Scots-Irish roots and a mind for business affairs, Mr. Whaley was born on October 5, 1823, in New York City. His family immigrated to Plymouth, Massachusetts, in 1722. Interestingly, Alexander Whaley, Thomas's great-grandfather, was a gunsmith who involved himself in the Boston Tea Party and the Revolutionary War. It was Thomas's father who operated as part of the New York Militia during the War of 1812.

In his father's will, it stated that Thomas Jr. should have the right to a decent education. After his studies at the Washington Institute, he took over management of his father's civic matters in 1846. He then commenced a new business journey, seeking employment with the Sutton & Company shipbuilding firm. In 1848, the unearthing of gold in California, plus the brand new alleged line of government steamships to California, ignited intrigue in his organization. With plans to extend the workforce to the Golden State, resulting in an office in San Francisco and a subsequent company partnership, Mr. Whaley finally made the decision to move to the west coast. On January 1, 1849, the young businessman embarked on the *Sutton* for a journey around Cape Horn. After 204 days at sea, he finally arrived in San Francisco.

Along with George Wardle, Thomas Whaley set up a store on Montgomery Street with the prime purpose of selling hardware and woodwork from his family's business, Whaley & Pye, in New York. He also presented utensils and mining gear on consignment. In April 1851, Thomas bought property at Rincon point and subsequently assembled a two-story home that boasted scenic views of the bay. The same year, when an arson-caused fire destroyed his business in San Francisco, young Mr. Whaley relocated to Old Town, San Diego, California, on October 4. Continuing with his business affairs, he opened up several businesses with Franklin, Ephraim Morse, Francis Hinton, and his brother Henry. Devoted to his civic affairs, he even learned to speak Spanish so he could conduct business with the local people of the town, having a population census at the time of 250–300 individuals. In August 1857, Mr. Whaley instituted his general store at the massive home, but its location was too far from the town's center, so he strategically relocated his business on the Plaza.

As Franklin and Whaley were conducting commercial affairs in their premiere store, the chief of the Luiseño tribe, Antonio Garra, had other plans. In November 1851, Mr. Garra and other tribes caused a revolt when the town sheriff announced he was going to commence the collection of taxes from those who operated cattle ranches. There were just a few remaining men and sentinels left to safely block against the raid of the Luiseño Indians. Thus, San Diego was ordered to go under martial law, where every man became a soldier. Eventually Garra was captured, and on January 10, 1852, his life was abruptly ended by firing squad. Thomas Whaley was one of the twelve-member squadron.

After the execution the town of San Diego returned to normal. That March, Franklin and Hinton decided not to do business together anymore. The following month Whaley joined forces with Francis Hinton, and they ran the successful "Tienda General." In fact, in the first year alone they profited $18,600, with sales averaging around $150 per day. Now Thomas Whaley had made enough money to go back east to marry the love of his life. In a letter to his mother while sailing on the *Sutton* Thomas imparted:

> You might call on Mrs. Lannay; you will find her a very pleasant lady. I may as well inform you that I have a particular regard for her youngest daughter, Miss Anna; indeed I love her and intend marrying her if ever I return from California a rich man . . . I may send for her. She is a pleasant and amiable young lady of very affectionate disposition and gentle and innocent as a lamb. She is only 16 or 17 years of age. You would no doubt love her as a daughter-in-law. She attends Miss Green's School on the 5th Avenue.

Whaley traveled to New York, to finally tie the knot on August 14, 1853, with French-born Anna Eloise De Lannay. The couple married at the Church of the Ascension in New York City. The groom brought his lady back to California, and they temporarily resided at the Gila House. A party was thrown the exact day of their arrival with dancing and music. In all, they became accustomed to the town's fiestas and other forms of entertainment.

It was customary to employ Native Americans as house servants, but Anna felt that they were difficult to discipline and hard to keep clothed. Mr. Whaley purchased a native girl from her parents for $100 worth of provisions from his store in return for the girl to live with the Whaley family. The young woman stayed with the family for a few weeks, then ran away, ultimately returning to her parents. The girl's mother and father consented to letting her go again, but again wanted to be paid. Mr. Whaley obliged and this process continued for some time.

Another infamous historical event occurred on August 17, 1852, when Yankee Jim Robinson was captured and subsequently found guilty of grand larceny. Mr. Robinson served as his own attorney during his trial, in which Judge John Hays presided. After the members of the jury deliberated for about thirty minutes, he received the death penalty by hanging on September 18, 1852. The verdict read as follows:

> Your jurors in the within case of James Robinson [Yankee Jim's real name] have the honor to return a verdict of guilty and do therefore sentence him to be hanged by the neck until dead.

Thomas Whaley was present at Yankee Jim's brutal hanging on September 18, and some say that the execution took place on the exact spot where the house stands today. Due to his tall height, Yankee Jim's neck did not break during the fall, and instead he slowly strangled to his last breath. Mr. Robinson is said to spiritually reside in the Greek-revival mansion today. Sadly, some, including myself, say that he is not resting in peace, as he is still upset about the ultimate verdict that cost him his life. (You will hear more about this in following chapters.)

The Whaley family had several children. Francis Hinton, born on December 28, 1854, was the couple's first child, and was named after one of Whaley's business partners. Thomas Whaley Jr. was born in August 1856. He tragically passed away at the tender age of seventeen months on January 29, 1858. Born in the Whaley home, Anna Amelia became the couple's third child on June 27, 1858. George Hay Ringgold Whaley was welcomed on November 5, 1860. On October 4, 1862, Violet Eloise was born, with Corinne Lillian arriving in San Francisco on September 4, 1864.

After the death of Thomas Jr. and another arson fire that destroyed Mr. Whaley's Plaza business, the family moved to San Francisco. In spring 1859, Thomas was given an appointment as Commissary Storekeeper, USA under Capt. M. D. L. Simpson, where he stayed for six years. On July 31, 1867, the office of the Quartermaster in San Francisco gave out orders to Mr. Whaley to travel to Sitka, Alaska Territory. With the responsibility of being in control of five carpenters, along with Quartermaster Department staff, he was to form a base of operations and set up stores. Thus, he was given orders to travel by the barque *Buena Vista* and take possession of the territory for the United States. Whaley then hoisted up the American flag and was then elected by ninety-four votes to the Council at Sitka, Alaska.

During this time Anna and the children sojourned in San Francisco, with Mary Condy Ringgold, the wife and widow of Lt. Col. George Ringgold, one of Thomas's friends. George and Mary had five children: three boys and two girls. Augustus S. Ensworth was entrusted with the task of looking over the Whaley business in San Diego during the family's absence. On May 27, 1862, San Diego was rocked by an earthquake, ultimately causing damage to many houses, including the Whaley family home. Upon the family's return to San Diego, Thomas then commenced remodeling work on his massive residence. Repairs were made to the home's front, as well as renovations to accommodate for the needs of five children.

Throughout history, the Whaley family home has been host to a variety of activities. Throughout the years there were many musical soirees, formal balls, and other parties. One of the upstairs rooms was reserved for Tanner troupe theater productions. On November 1, 1868, Mr. Whaley leased the second floor of his house and the usage of the corral to Thomas W. Tanner for $20 gold coin. On August 12, 1869, the county leased the home for two years to serve as a courtroom. Also included was the use of the three upstairs rooms for county record storage. With the rent being $65.00 per month, Thomas H. Bush became one of its first judges. Political meetings ensued there, and it later became the courtroom of Edward H. Burr and Francis Hinton Whaley. Furthermore, this spacious northward room was also utilized as a billiard hall, dairy, kindergarten, Sunday school, store, and residence.

Once competition commenced for Old Town and New Town, Thomas Whaley offered to sell his building to the county, but the board did not take any action. A July 14, 1870, *Union* newspaper article relayed that the Board of Supervisors passed an order which directed the removal of the county records from the Whaley mansion to the Express building in New Town. Furthermore, Horton's Hall became the future meeting site for the court system.

In the evening hours of March 31, 1871, Chalmers Scott and his friends took a couple express wagons over to the Whaley House and broke into the courtroom with the purpose of removing the records. They then took them over to Sixth and G Streets, where they were stored in the Wells Fargo building's second floor. Supervisors then informed an unhappy Mr. Whaley that they would no longer be monetarily responsible for paying rent once the building was empty. In a series of letters written to the board, Mr. Whaley pointed out that their lease had not yet expired, and thus the county was responsible for paying rent until the lease was up. Disconcerted, Thomas also demanded money and repairs to his structure. The board paid little attention to Whaley, thus signifying the end of Old Town's reign over political associations. The power torch had transferred its hands over to New Town.

Thomas Whaley, along with his civic partner, Philip Crosthwaite, relocated to New Town; however, their business was not successful. Thomas then traveled to New York, to settle his father's estate. It was not until 1879, that he came back to San Diego. Once he was back in Southern California, he joined forces with E. W. Morse and C. P. Noell and developed a real estate firm. He eventually retired in 1888.

On January 5, 1882, the Whaley's daughter, Violet Eloise, was married to George T. Bertolacci in Old Town by Rev. Dr. Bunker, followed by the marriage of Anna Amelia and John Thomas Whaley (first cousin and Henry Hurst Whaley's son). After a year and three months of marriage Violet divorced George, ultimately causing her to become very depressed. Sadly, this led to her committing suicide by shooting herself in the chest. After she shot herself Thomas brought her inside the parlor, where she passed away. In the inquisition by the coroner's jury Thomas Whaley said:

> I think at about half past six. I sprang immediately forward and went to the water closet back of the house, knowing the sound came from there. I found her, Violet, sitting upon the lower seats of the water closet. I took her into my arms and carried her from there into the house. As I entered the back door I called to her mother, saying: Mama, Violet has shot herself! I brought her into the back parlor and laid her upon the lounge.

In November 1885, the family erected a one-story residence on Whaley property near the junction of E. and State Streets which became the family's home for many years. Thomas also became a city trustee in 1885, and served as a notary public. On December 14, at age sixty-seven, he passed away at his home on State Street. The stately mansion that he built slowly started to decay as the years went by. It was not forgotten, as in 1956, the City of San Diego's Board of Supervisors all agreed to buy and restore the Greek-revival historical structure to its original condition. In a way, I feel that this decision was bittersweet for Thomas, as he was always so proud of his home. Perhaps he never really got over Old Town's political losses, but was able to regain some dignity and happiness knowing that his house continues to stand tall and proud in modern time.

As you read through this section, it is hard not to believe that the Whaley House is claimed to be one of the most, if not the most, hauntingly active former residences in the United States. Countless people from all ages, cultures, and walks of life have encountered the ghosts and spirits that reside in and claim the 1857 Greek-revival mansion as their home. From Yankee Jim Robinson to Thomas Whaley himself, various types of paranormal activity consistently occur inside the walls of the famed edifice on San Diego Avenue. Apparitional sightings, disembodied vocalizations, cold spots, and the like occur here, and if you are intrigued at all by the spiritual realm, this historic home is the spot for you.

The historical events surrounding the home's history are probably the greatest foundation for its haunting events. Still, there may be other prevailing reasons why the people of its fabled past continue to make themselves known through the veil. Many questions go unanswered, even though research continues to make attempts at answering them. Why does the Whaley family, in spirit form, continue to commune with the living? Are they here by choice, or do they have some sort of unfinished business? Are they acting as ethereal tour guides for the thousands of people who visit their home each month? What message(s) do they impart? The list of questions goes on. Anyone should feel honored should they come in contact with one of the spirits of the Whaley House. Remember to be reverent and respectful, as the historic structure ultimately belongs to the Whaley family.

Many visitors to the home describe the feeling of being watched and acquire general creepy vibes. Theresa Cannizzaro shared that she feels its spiritual inhabitants are curious about the mortal realm's intent for visiting the location. The house seems to unearth a general heaviness, especially when it is less crowded with tourists.

One of my fellow investigators had a profound intuitive experience in the room known as Violet's quarters. Even though it is labeled as such, this room never solely belonged to Violet; however, this does not diminish people's experiences. While looking into its premises, my colleague felt a pervasive feeling of sadness, so much so that it caused her to cry and hurry out of the home. Was she tapping into Violet's own depressive moods? Several years ago, while conducting an EVP session in the home, I somehow captured the spirit voice of a young woman saying, "Violet hurts . . ." My heart immediately ached upon hearing this, and it made me wonder if Violet is reliving her depression even in ethereal form. Since Violet experienced a lot of despair and dejection, could it be that her energy has somehow psychically imprinted itself on to the property?

Many people have supernatural occurrences in the courtroom. Theresa shared that she has captured colored orbs hovering over the witness stand. Most often dismissing orbs as having a logical explanation, she went on to say that these particular ones emanated their own energy and appeared in blue and red tones. One of the fables associated with the Whaley House is that a portal or spiritual passageway exists in one of the jury boxes. Whether this is true or not, it is evident that the courtroom seems to be a hot bed of activity.

Some visitors have experienced the sensation of being touched. Theresa shared with me that someone invisible to the naked eye pulled the hair on top of her head as she was walking on a pathway behind the home. She ruled out running into above tree branches and to this day has not come up with a logical explanation for this occurrence. The family's dog, Dolly, is known to interact with guests in spirit form, occasionally brushing up or licking peoples' legs. Others have heard her bark and have seen her wandering in various areas of the house.

An employee recently shared with me some of the otherworldly experiences he has had with the spirits of the home. One morning, as he was preparing to open up the house for visitors, he noticed a figure as he was ascending the stairs. Out of the corner of his eye he noticed pant legs and a man staring at him through the railings.

Positioned in front of the back of the upstairs bedroom door, the ethereal presence appeared in a black-and-white tone and looked to be in his '20s. Familiar with Thomas Whaley's distinctive facial features, the employee knew he was looking at Mr. Whaley's spirit form. Intriguingly, he also described an unusual characteristic of the apparition: He said that the hands were abnormally proportioned really wide on the staircase railings. He felt that the home's patriarchal figure was looking on him with a gaze of curiosity.

Cynthia Wilson commenced her job as a Whaley House docent on October 18, 2008. She is one of the known staff members who has experienced a lot of ghostly energy at the Whaley House. I was fortunate to be able to conduct an interview with her inside the edifice's renowned courtroom, as she has a plethora of supernatural encounters during her tenure as a docent.

Known as the "Whaley House Ghost Magnet," Cynthia has experienced a lot of disembodied voices and apparitional sightings. She even recalled how ghostly forms have been seen on the home's balconies. On one of her tours, she felt the movement as Dolly tugged on the bottom of her dress. Since the dog appears frequently in ghost form, Cynthia has described her apparition to appear as a darting white mass. She has also heard Dolly's disembodied vocalization and describes it as a sound echoing from a far off dimension.

Cynthia describes the ghostly energy as a general "heaviness," especially when the supernatural activity is really strong. This is when she advises her tour guests to start snapping photographs, as several anomalous pictures have been captured throughout the years at the Whaley House. She went on to explain how a tall, skeletal figure has appeared beside her in photographs as she was hosting her tours of the home.

Furthermore, Cynthia also shared how a phantom little girl's vocalization can be heard on various audio recorders, possibly associated with a child by the name of Marion Reynolds, Thomas and Anna's great-granddaughter, who tragically perished in 1912. She resided in the Whaley House for many years. Cynthia said that blue orb sightings in the house are connected to Marion's spirit. In her own words, Cynthia describes her very first paranormal encounter as a docent of the Whaley House:

> My very first experience was the night that I had my first shift. I was unaware that everyone had left the house, as they were waiting for me on the front porch. So all that we had was a light that was downstairs through the open doors. As I came down, after I realized I had changed out of my period attire, I was alone, which was kind of creepy. At the staircase, as I turned, I saw that we had a velvet rope that divides the parlor and the study. The study rope lifted up slowly and held there for a few seconds. Then everyone was looking through the window and saw that the rope was swinging wildly of its own volition. It didn't feel cold

as I went up to touch it. That was my first paranormal experience here.

Then there is Yankee Jim Robinson, one of the most well-known ghostly inhabitants of the home. Even Mr. Whaley had an experience with his ghost shortly after Jim was hung on the property. In *Tales of Old Town*, the author describes how participants experienced otherworldly events while reenacting the trial and execution of Robinson in 1966. Many of them documented strange occurrences, such as abnormal upstairs noises and the sound of heavy boots walking around. One night while in the home I asked Jim to make himself known. Immediately I heard hard-pressed phantom sounds of boots meandering around upstairs. Was this my imagination, or did I actually encounter Yankee Jim's spirit form? One individual even saw a man standing on the upstairs landing. We know that Mr. Whaley has been seen in ethereal form in this exact spot; however, could Yankee Jim spiritually appear in this location as well?

Francis Hinton Whaley also makes appearances from time to time. The consensus is that he enjoys the visitors that come through his home. Remember that he used to offer tours of his house back in the day. Researchers who are familiar with the home's haunted happenings feel that Francis is intrigued by the modern-day electronic devices used in ghost investigations. Apparently, his favorite gadget is the camera. In fact, many people report camera malfunctions in the home, or document a picture seemingly being taken of its own volition. One night, as I was looking into the kitchen from the outside, I felt a breath against my left ear, which was accompanied by a disembodied male voice saying, "Hi." Intuitively I felt this was Francis Hinton Whaley, making his rounds to the guests visiting his home.

So we are left with questions as to why places such as the Whaley House become so paranormally active. History plays a substantial part in creating a foundation for ghostly activity. History and spiritual events share a deep kinship, and you really cannot have one without the other. They complement each other beautifully. Since the Whaley House is considered an epithet for San Diego history, it would make sense that it continues to share its legends and lore in modern time with visitors from all over the world. For those wishing to study the theories into why paranormal phenomena cross the threshold of the spiritual world into our physical world, then places such as the Whaley House provide the backdrop for our mortal realm to communicate with those of our past.

The Whaley House, on the corner of San Diego Avenue and Harney Street, is a testament to the sheer courage of one of San Diego's leading pioneer families. Mr. Whaley's prophetic words—"My new house, when completed, will be the handsomest, most comfortable and convenient place in town or within 150 miles of here . . ."—have truly come to pass and continue to echo in the heart and soul of visitors today. When you visit Old Town, please take some time and visit the Whaley home, as it speaks of its bygone era and continues to share the stories of its colorful past.

PART IV:
Julian's Most Haunted

Southern California is home to one of the nation's most historically quaint mining towns. About an hour or so drive from Central San Diego, Julian is nestled among beautiful rolling hills and mountains. Noted for its award-winning apple pie, the small town boasts various gift and antique stores, delectable restaurants, and of course, ghosts. In addition to its abundant history and welcoming atmosphere, perhaps its geography can possibly explain why many of its former residents choose to remain in the present day.

Chapter 10: Julian History

In 1869, the town of Julian, California, was founded during a gold strike. Approximately 600 people inhabited the region soon after the unearthing of gold. Julian differed from normal mining towns, in that it became a bustling community, ultimately attracting many tourists from all walks of life. In its original days, Julian saw an eclectic mix of ethnicities, including individuals of English, Polish, Welsh, Jewish, African American, and Italian heritage. In fact, women and their families contributed to the everlasting success of Julian as a community. Between 1870 and 1880, the small mountain town saw the development of two hotels, two cafes, five stores, two blacksmith shops, two livery stables, and many saloons. The native people worked on road-building projects and sold fruits and vegetables to local miners.

Local legend holds that the Native Americans in the region knew about the area's gold deposits but kept it to themselves. A former slave by the name of Fred Coleman was also said to have discovered gold deposits while tending to his horse. It was then that he noticed reflective matter in the water and immediately informed the Coleman mining district and Emily City mining town. As one can imagine, word of gold in the region spread like wildfire.

During that same year, four cousins from Georgia landed themselves in Temecula. While traveling through the Cuyamaca mountains to Arizona, Drury and James Bailey and Mike and Webb Julian decided to settle in the area. In 1870, two distinct gold deposits were found near their camp base. The four men later founded the Julian Mining district on February 15, 1870, as a way to safeguard the increasing amount of miners in the town. Mike Julian was appointed the town's first district recorder. Interestingly, the cousins decided to name the town after Mike, as they felt that the name "Julian" sounded much more appealing than the name "Bailey."

Once the *San Diego Union Tribune* ran news about gold deposits in the region, people started flocking to the area to control the gold mines. As time went on proceedings took place to determine the legal access to the mines. These proceedings were an attempt to change the boundaries of the Cuyamaca Grant as a way to include the gold fields within property owners' lines. On May 25, 1870, grant owners had a business meeting as a way to negotiate with Julian miners. Mining efforts could continue as long as royalties were issued to the grant owners for any removed gold deposits. These men were opposed to this compromise due to the fact that some mines would be heavily taxed, up to fifty percent of their wages.

In the end, landowners were not able to change the boundaries of the Cuyamaca land grants and include gold fields within their property. On April 5, 1871, J. R. Hardenbergh, the new US Surveyor General for California, closed the case without altering the grant boundaries. In the end the miners triumphed, and the entire town of Julian rejoiced in the decision. President Ulysses S. Grant permitted the authorized land grant boundaries on December 19, 1874.

As mentioned, several families that came to the region decided to stay in the area due to its agricultural significance. The first schoolhouse opened its doors to the town's resident children in 1870. Many women supervised their own hotels and/or boarding houses for the mining men. Margaret Tull Robinson managed Hotel Robinson with her husband Albert. After her husband's passing, Mrs. Robinson handled the hotel duties until the Jacobs family bought the property around 1919.

The town's residents formed supportive and caring relationships with each other, again a testament to Julian's overall success as a community. Indeed, Julian was a viable mixture of various ethnicities ultimately contributing to a successful business community. In fact, boarding houses and hotels catered to Julian's thriving population. Prior to this people lived in tents in what was known as Emily City. The town acquired its first bank in September 1870.

Traveling back and forth to San Diego helped business affairs in the mining town. Joseph Yancey moved to Julian in 1870, to raise horses. He utilized his animals to transport provisions between Julian and San Diego. Chester Gunn ran a pony express mail service between the two areas. This method was gradually replaced by stages, as they could travel back and forth in a single day.

The population of Julian dwindled to about one hundred people after gold was discovered in adjacent Arizona and Nevada. In 1881, the Julian and Banner mining districts merged into the new Julian district. The founding of the Gold King and Gold Queen mines in 1888, improved the town's business affairs. Additionally, apple and pear orchards were quite prolific in the region. In the 1870s, Madison and Thomas Brady were credited with the planting of the first apple trees in Julian. In fact, once the mining days waned in the 1890s, agriculture was next in line, contributing to the town's continued survival.

Close friendships and an active social life had a direct affect on Julian's success. Social gatherings evolving around dancing were extremely popular. In 1909, the premiere Apple Day festival was held to celebrate the year's harvest and a "new stage in the life of Julian." People from neighboring towns Poway, Ramona, and Escondido joined the happy residents of Julian for various social affairs, such as barbecues, horse and relay races, and dancing.

Today, one can visit the town of Julian and its historical buildings and be reminded of its days past. This historic mining town experiences all of the four seasons—a rarity for the City of San Diego. People from all over the nation come to visit this location on an annual basis, enjoying its gorgeous mountain ambience. Plenty of outdoor activities are available in and around Julian, including hiking, fishing, and sightseeing. Additionally, Julian is popular for retreats and weddings. Of course, this historic town is prized for its delectable apples and apple pies. Being that Julian is a former mining town during the California Gold Rush, it is not a surprise that it has a lot of history.

With all of its historical significance, one can see why the town of Julian also boasts paranormal activity from time to time. I have come into contact with several residents who have encountered strange happenings. The spirits of its past continue to share their story in modern time. Perhaps Julian's residents are continuing on with their duties from years ago. While people can experience ghostly activity in any area of the town, there are certain locations that are more widely known for their spiritual phenomena than others. The former Hotel Robinson (now called the Julian Hotel), Julian Pioneer Cemetery, and neighboring Pine Hills Lodge are three hot spot areas in this region.

Chapter 11:
The Pine Hills Lodge

The front entrance to the rustic Pine Hills Lodge. This site is an ongoing paranormal research project for the San Diego Paranormal Research Society.

Pine Hills, once the gathering place of San Diego County's socially elite, continues to offer excellent accommodations in a rustic setting. At the turn of the century, the lodge was originally built as a romantic hideaway in the mountains amongst the surrounding apple orchards and forests. The history of the lodge is a fascinating part of its unique ambience. It is a perfect getaway for anyone wishing to have a break from city life and surround themselves in the beauty and serenity of Julian's mountain landscape.

The Pine Hills Lodge was built in 1912, by Col. Ed Fletcher, a prominent real estate developer and banker in San Diego. It was designed by world-famous architect Richard Requa, known for many of the structures in San Diego's Balboa Park and Zoo. The bark-on wood log construction is considered irreplaceable and was done by builder Charles Engebretson.

In August 1925, the lodge was sold to Fred A. Sutherland, owner and operator of Sutherland Stage and Yellow Cab. He was a friend of Jack Dempsey, the prize-winning professional boxer. Sutherland built a gym at the lodge and convinced Dempsey to come to the site to train for his second fight against Gene Tunney. On September 23, 1926, Dempsey lost the fight, but the gym he trained in remains standing to this day.

Over the years the fitness center was used as a local movie theater. In the era of the 1920s–1940s, cabins and treehouses were built to accommodate the demand for more guests visiting the property. The treehouses are now gone. In 1980, the new owner, Dave Goodman, transformed the gym into a dinner theater for local amateur productions of known plays. After a twenty-three-year run, the theater closed in 2004, as demand had waned. Since the purchase in 1998, major renovations have been completed, restoring the "famous Lodge" to its former splendor. In July 2003, the lodge was acquired by new owners who planned to continue its legacy of rustic ambience. Under new management, the building staff aspires to rekindle a reputation for delectable foods, gregarious service, and above all, a genuine feeling of tranquility and amicable hospitality—a step back in time to a romantic hideaway.

The San Diego Paranormal Research Society (SDPRS) first learned of the lodge's haunted history in 2011. While hosting a paranormal research presentation at the San Diego History Center, the team was able to meet Mrs. Sheldon, the current owner of the lodge. Subsequently, she asked the team to come out to the bucolic site to conduct ghost research on the property. Since that time the team has conducted several overnight paranormal research investigations on the premises.

Like many other haunted locations, Pine Hills Lodge has a wide array of paranormal claims, ranging from apparitional sightings and disembodied voices and footsteps to a general eerie feeling of unseen eyes watching your every move. Additionally, the geology of Julian's mountains contains quartzite, limestone, and other geological attributes known to retain spiritual energy. Furthermore, Ley Lines can possibly explain why some locations are spiritual highways and Julian is no exception, as many Ley Lines run straight through the town and its adjacent mountains and hills.

From reading the brochure, one is aware that Mr. Dempsey utilized the gym as a practice location for his boxing. The gym was also used as a theater for various plays. There is a theory that postulates why theaters are known to have ghostly energy: It is because of the vast array of emotions felt from hundreds of people, which seem to have an everlasting stay at their respective location. It is theorized that ghosts and spirits thrive on these various emotions to manifest and communicate with the living. Could this be one of the reasons why the gym-turned-theater at Pine Hills Lodge houses paranormal activity?

There is another reason—a sad one in fact—why this particular area may house ghostly energy: An accident occurred during Dempsey's reign when a large wooden beam fell down and instantly killed a worker. On both of our investigations we have communicated with a male energy inside the structure. It is our sincere hope that this male energy finds peace and moves on to where he needs to be. Perhaps he has already done so.

Additionally, it has been said that a male writer committed suicide while staying overnight in one of the adjacent lodges. Interestingly, while on my first investigation of the lodge in 2011, I was getting a strong intuitive impression of a death in the same proximity to where the man was said to have passed away. At the time of my impression I was not yet aware of the possible death. Mrs. Sheldon later told me about the writer. We are currently trying to verify the veracity of said incident.

Each member of the SDPRS team has also experienced high strangeness in the projection booth area of the former theater. We have all seen the residual sighting of a shadow figure repetitively walking past the projection window on numerous occasions. We have since tried to recreate this phenomenon to see if there is some logical explanation, but to no avail. Intuitive impressions suggest this entity is the ethereal form of a past projectionist who loved his job at the theater.

Another interesting phenomenon that surrounds this structure is the consistent knocking sounds heard while inside its premises. We have investigated this occurrence only to discover that it is not a phenomenon at all, but the natural sounds of acorns hitting the structure or woodpeckers pecking on the outside walls. In the morning after our investigation we actually witnessed a woodpecker doing its thing, and the sound was one hundred percent reminiscent of the knocking noise we heard during the previous night's research.

We have concluded that this gym-turned-theater houses paranormal activity that is both intelligent and residual in nature. It is definitely considered a "hot spot" on the property. We do not have a lot of tangible evidence from this particular structure, as most of our experiences are subjective in nature. However, SDPRS member Ali Schreiber captured a very strange anomaly in one of her photographs taken from inside the projection booth. We have conducted various experiments to try and recreate the phenomenon and have not yet found a logical explanation. We are currently in the process of having photographic specialists analyze it, as their expertise may lead to a natural explanation. Regardless of the lack of tangible data, we will say this so-called hot spot definitely has some mysterious, high strangeness going on.

As far as the main lodge, which also includes a restaurant and pub, paranormal activity seems to be centered upstairs, where the rooms are located. On numerous occasions, the owners and their staff have heard disembodied voices and footsteps. While upstairs, and especially while in Room 6, people have seen the peripheral sighting of a shadow figure walking down the hall. One of the cleaning crew also attested to this phenomenon, as she described her sighting of a tall dark figure as it walked past the door. On one particular research project I stayed in Room 6 and discussed seeing the identical figure out of my peripheral vision while unpacking equipment. There are speculations that this figure is the ethereal form of a past lodge owner.

Interestingly, vacationers have also smelled the phantom scent of smoke while upstairs in their rooms. It must be noted that the upstairs portion of the main lodge experienced a fire during the 1930s or 1940s. Could these phantom smells be the residual imprints of the fire that occurred? We had a guest investigator with us during our most recent investigation. Toward the end of our project, we decided to do some EVP sessions in Room 3, which is where one of the past owners stayed while running the lodge. Room 3 is situated directly across from the room that caught fire many years ago. Our guest investigator, Gina, experienced acute coughing attacks during our EVP work in Room 3 that only improved once she left the room. Was Gina's body tapping into the residual energy left over from the fire?

During our EVP session we had two recorders and a video camera running, and we captured two interesting audio pieces: 1) a male voice saying, "Hello"; and 2) a response to my (Nicole) statement about us being willing to help relay a message to family members or friends, which sounds like, "Let Me Go" or "Let Me Know." On our investigations we always offer to help the energies and let them know that we can relay their message, should they have one to offer.

Instrumental Trans Communication (ITC) is considered live two-way communication between the living and deceased. The SDPRS team has conducted several ITC sessions at the Pine Hills Lodge with some interesting results. A strong example of intelligent spirit communication also occurred in Room 3 of the main lodge. As an experiment I asked, "Can you tell us the name of the current lodge owner?" Intriguingly, a male response, "Hannah," can be deciphered about five seconds after my question—and Hannah is Mrs. Sheldon's first name.

The restaurant seating area in the main lodge is the site of a former Native American village, so the residual anomalous sounds emanating from this area may be the historical replay of days past. Interestingly, while conducting EVP work in the dining room area, SDPRS members have documented hearing audible female vocalizations directly stemming from the portion of the dining room that is said to have been the tribe's kitchen area. People have also heard the vocalization of a little girl. To this day we are not sure if this little ethereal energy originates from the lodge days or prior to the building of the entire structure.

Some of the other adjacent structures on the property have also experienced paranormal activity. Again, disembodied voices, footsteps, and audible noise phenomena have been witnessed. However, the energy seems playful and curious. The SDPRS team continues to conduct historical and paranormal research at the picturesque lodge. If you are in the mood to stay in a rustic ambience in the company of a ghost or two the Pine Hills Lodge is the place for you.

Chapter 12: Julian Hotel

When you visit the historic mining town of Julian, make sure to stay a night or two at the quaint Julian Hotel. You may have an encounter with one of its spirits.

One famous piece of Julian's history centers on the Robinson Hotel, a picturesque cottage situated right in the center of town. Albert and Margaret Robinson earned a solid reputation after building this hotel in 1887. They operated the edifice for twenty-eight years, until Albert's death in 1915. After his passing the hotel changed its name to the Julian Hotel. Margaret later sold the historic hotel for $1,500.

Visitors who step inside this hotel will be transported back in time. It is the oldest running hotel in southern California. In 1869, Albert and Margaret Robinson came to Julian shortly after gold was discovered. Albert did his duties as a freed slave, and it was during this time that he met his wife, Margaret. The couple eventually married and began building the Julian Hotel. The couple soon became famous around the town, and various famous people have stayed at the hotel. After Mr. Robinson's death, his wife presided over the building until 1921, then sold it to a popular mining engineer, Martin Jacobs.

This discussion of Julian would not be complete without sharing a little of the ghostly phenomena that take place in this town. It has been said that Albert and Margaret Robinson are still roaming the grounds of their hotel, perhaps making sure it is still being operated to their liking. Footsteps have been heard descending from the second floor. Room 10 of the structure used to be Albert's room. People who visit the hotel have occasionally reported seeing Albert's ethereal form. Cold spots, footsteps, the feeling of being watched, and the occasional smell of pipe smoke are sensed. One maid even saw phantom pipe smoke behind her as she was cleaning. Maids have made beds only to find them unmade minutes later. Furthermore, furniture is found to be moved throughout the hotel.

Other odd phenomena have been reported as well. A hotel guest documented that she felt extremely weird and then visualized an image that suddenly appeared to her. She described it as resembling a person without any concrete features. High strangeness exists at this iconic building, including great balls of fire seen traveling through the rooms. This may be more reminiscent of odd light anomalies. Glass would break and furniture would move about of its own volition. Much of this psychokinetic activity has ceased in recent years.

When visiting Julian, do not just stop for the apple pie. Make sure to stay in the Julian Hotel. Who knows, Albert may pay you a visit. The warm hospitality that the hotel provides is an indication of why Albert may choose to remain in the structure he so loved.

Chapter 13: Julian's Haven of Rest (Pioneer Cemetery)

> Primitive living conditions, violence, alcohol, disease, and fatal accidents, all common in the Julian gold mining district, created an urgent need for a graveyard. Such use began on this then private property with the burial of stillborn babies under a sheltering oak tree. The earliest burials recorded are those of two teenage boys who died in the winter of 1875. Soon other victims were buried, some with "their boots on" in unmarked graves, some in family plots and some alone in what became, in fact, a community cemetery.
>
> –Julian Historical Society, Pioneer Cemetery 1870 Plaque

Julian's Haven of Rest Cemetery lies just west of its downtown commercial businesses. It is situated on a hill in a peaceful yet tranquil setting. The many indigenous oak trees, combined with a variety of headstones, almost give this quaint setting an ominous feel at night. It is unsure whether anyone managed its confines from the time of its first burial up to the 1923 founding of the Julian Cemetery Association.

Early Julian residents lived a rough life, where miners argued on a consistent basis. In fact, the historic town was witness to seven murders during the 1870s. It has been said that many other men passed away from alcohol poisoning or accidents in the mines. Records indicate that one of the first persons interred was in 1875, with the death of Tommie Harrall, a wood chopper crushed by a falling tree. Drury Bailey, who played a vital role in the overall development of Julian, is also buried in the cemetery.

There are many Julian pioneers interred in this cemetery on a hill. On the markers you can see the names of settlers, such as the Putnams, Scotts, and Wilcoxes, who traveled to Julian for mining purposes. People remained in this historic town for a variety of other reasons. The McCains operated a blacksmith shop, as well as the Mountain Glen Hotel. Former slave America Newton arrived in 1872, and settled on some land two miles west of Julian. The Hoskings, who originally traveled to the town for health reasons, also operated the Julian Hotel. This family also donated part of the land for the cemetery. These families, as well as the Robinsons and others, are laid to rest in this quaint burial ground.

Cemeteries are known to be hot spot locations for supernatural activity. Some of the common claims of paranormal occurrences include apparitional sightings, cold spots, disembodied vocalizations, and unusual light anomalies. I have talked to Julian residents who claim that ghostly activity occurs at many sites throughout the historic mining town, with the Haven of Rest being one of those places.

Since I do not believe in conducting paranormal research projects in cemeteries I have not investigated the Haven of Rest. I have talked with some people who have had odd encounters while visiting its grounds. I chatted with one person who visited the cemetery at night with his wife. She started to sense the presence of ethereal energy and simultaneously they both witnessed odd light activity. Whether it was a natural phenomenon or something otherworldly, it was intriguing that they experienced a psychic impression possibly followed by something supernatural.

Other witnesses have described seeing fleeting apparitions and hearing disembodied vocalizations throughout its premises. Since Julian is a relatively small town, it is possible that some of the reported voices emanate from living persons, as noise travels through the wind. Other people, including those who have conducted paranormal research work inside the cemetery's confines, have documented capturing EVPs—alleged spirit talk that is not heard at the time of capture. Whether the Haven of Rest is haunted remains to be seen; however, since Julian is purported to have supernatural events, it is possible that its cemetery does, too.

PART V:
Downtown San Diego and Gaslamp Quarter District's Most Haunted

Downtown San Diego and its historic Gaslamp Quarter District boast various attractions, hotels, museums, night clubs, and award-winning restaurants that attract people from all over the world on an annual basis. Many of San Diego's world-renowned locations are situated just a short drive, walk, or bike ride from the many Victorian-era buildings and modern day high rises that make up this metropolis. Considered the pulsing artery of "America's Finest City," it is no wonder that ghosts and spirits inhabit many of its celebrated buildings. In this section, you will hear the tales of two noteworthy edifices where the chronicles of times gone by continue to be told in the present.

Chapter 14: Horton Grand Hotel

An elegant nineteenth-century boutique edifice, the Horton Grand Hotel sits in the heart of San Diego's Gaslamp Quarter District.

Boasting an impressive history, the Horton Grand Hotel sits in the heart of the Gaslamp District in downtown San Diego. It is actually a restoration of two distinct mid-1880s historic edifices: the Grant Horton Hotel and the Brooklyn-Kahle Saddlery Hotel, previously located where Horton Plaza Mall stands today. Original period items were utilized, such as nineteenth-century window glass. The grand structure's antiques came from around the world. The oak registration desk and the Palace Bar's bar area were brought from a church in New York.

Originally known as the Brooklyn Hotel, Khale Saddlery acquired its fame due to famous gunslinger Wyatt Earp, a well-known lawman who came to San Diego in 1886. To commemorate New Town's founder, Alonzo Horton, the hotel became known as the Horton Grand in 1907. The hotel's most lively times took place in the mid-1930s. From 1912, and for the following sixty-six years, the ground floor of the hotel was used for the Khale saddle store, a famous saddle and harness store that attracted western celebrities. The shop designed hand-carved tack and saddles for actors and rodeo notables.

Mr. Earp's brother persuaded him to look into the city's real estate boom. Known for being an astute trailblazer and explorer, he traveled from one boom town to another. Perhaps the hotel's most famous guest, Wyatt Earp sojourned its premises for seven years.

Colonel Ed Fletcher, a famous San Diego citizen, resided at the hotel during the 1890s. Fletcher is known for having developed East County locations such as Grossmont and Mount Helix. Furthermore, he also constructed the blueprints for the Del Mar area. The Fletcher Hills neighborhood and the street known as Fletcher Parkway were both named after the colonel.

Opening its doors in 1886, the Grand Horton Hotel was a stylish and ornate Italianate Victorian structure constructed by German immigrant Peter Mayerhofer. He built the elegant hotel due to his desire to replicate the Innsbruck Hotel in Austria. The hotel was part of 300 buildings erected during the boom of the 1880s, as a way to cater to the arrival of those wishing to visit and/or settle in San Diego at the time. In 1885, after the arrival of San Diego's premiere transcontinental railroad, more than 26,000 visitors came to the small town.

Today's Horton Grand Hotel is elegantly situated in an area that was once known as the heart of the city's replication of the Barbary Coast's Stingaree District. This neighborhood consisted of a combination of gambling halls, saloons, opium dens, and brothels mixed with a few legally justifiable commercial businesses. For many years this area remained the epicenter for unlawful activity.

In fact, Ida Bailey was the Stingaree's most popular and ostentatious individual. Her residence, known as the Canary Cottage, was near in proximity to where the Horton Grand's restaurant stands in modern time. Even though Ida was involved with illicit and promiscuous activities, her cottage served prized food and drinks.

In December 1912, the Stingaree District gradually dissipated, paving the pathway for the emergence of Chinatown, with Chinese immigrants encompassing approximately three percent of San Diego's populace at the time. For employment they worked as laborers, housekeepers, launderers, merchants, clerks, cooks, fishermen, and even physicians. Additionally, a Chinese boarding house was on the corner of 3rd and Island.

Each room of the Horton Grand displays its own type of character and charm. When you walk through its entrance doors, you can immediately feel the nostalgia associated with historic times. The hotel boasts a quaint and welcoming feeling, with its walls whispering about days gone by. With its rich history, it is no wonder the Horton Grand Hotel is known for its spiritual ambience. Hotels are said to attract supernatural happenings due to the many people who visit them and the many emotional imprints left behind. This lavish structure houses resident spirits, one of whom is Roger Whittaker, a gambler who was murdered in the mid-1800s.

Room 309 apparently houses the ethereal specter of Roger A. Whittaker, who so abruptly lost his life many years ago. Two psychics were brought into this room to investigate, where they learned that its resident ghost was that of Whittaker. According to these psychics, Whittaker was murdered in a different hotel, but chooses to remain in Room 309 because it is reminiscent of his old room.

Room 309 is very popular as far as paranormal activity is concerned. People have witnessed Whittaker's full-body apparition not only in his room, but also in other areas as well. Housekeeping staff has reported shaking beds, lights going on and off of their own volition, and a sense of being watched. An indentation of a man's body has been observed on the bed when no one was staying in the room. When various guests played music in the area, they subsequently reported drafts above their heads. Whittaker's ethereal form has also been known to move things around in the room. Many visitors have reported being touched by ghostly hands. One guest even reported being touched on the shoulder by a freezing hand.

There are intriguing experiences in Room 309 centering on the game of poker. In fact, there have been instances where cards have been moved to other parts of the location. Most astounding is when a group of guests heard the sound of a phantom poker game occurring with men dealing cards.

There are various theories for why Mr. Whittaker spiritually sojourns in the Horton Grand Hotel. Some say that after his untimely murder, his body was dumped in the vicinity of where Ida Bailey's property once stood. Another postulation suggests that he was cheating on a game of cards; he escaped and hid in Room 309, but was later shot and killed. Theory holds that perhaps when the hotel was relocated, he too switched to the new location and Room 309. Again, these are just theories, as no one really knows the answer to why Mr. Whittaker's ghost remains in the hotel.

In addition to the playful specter of Roger A. Whittaker, other areas of the hotel are also known to have paranormal activity. Phantom footsteps are reported in other rooms. An apparition dressed in western attire appeared before a guest and suddenly vanished before his very eyes. Could this be the ghost or spirit of Wyatt Earp? Ida Bailey's spirit is also known to haunt the premises. Perhaps she is still playing out the days when she owned the Canary Cottage.

In my opinion, the staircase leading up to the various floors and rooms gives off an eerie vibe. One evening, as I visited the hotel, I noticed movement out of my peripheral vision on the second story landing. When I directly glanced at what I was visually spotting, I noticed a humanoid shadow figure. The entire experience lasted about a second or so. Intriguingly, other people have noticed odd visual sightings on the ornate stairs. An example of this is when a hotel guest witnessed a group of 1880s-clad spirits traveling down this exact wooden flight of stairs.

Remember that the general area where the Horton Grand sits was home to saloons, opium dens, gambling parlors, and brothels. With this type of history, it is no wonder that some folks from long ago have decided to stay. Much of the spiritual energy is most likely a historical imprint from the hotel's various time periods. Thus, paranormal occurrences in this category are absent of intelligence and consciousness. They typically replay at relevant time periods, such as anniversaries. Furthermore, the hotel's renovations could have increased ghostly energy at the site. When I have visited this historic edifice, I immediately feel like I was placed in the middle of the late 1800s.

Chapter 15: William Heath Davis House (The Davis-Horton House)

When people talk of early day San Diego pioneers, William Heath Davis typically comes up in the conversation. With his intelligent brain for business and his amicable personality, Mr. Davis was one of the most well-respected individuals in California prior to the Gold Rush days. Known as "Kanaka Bill" by shipmates, Davis was a thriving merchant in San Francisco and had extensive trading experience in San Diego. As a ten-year-old in 1831, Mr. Davis made his premiere visit to California from Hawaii via Sitka aboard the *Louisa*, a liner returning to Honolulu from San Diego. Two years later, he went to San Diego yet again and re-visited in 1838, aboard the *Don Quixote*. He continued his travels to California's southernmost city in the 1840s, marrying into the Estudillo family of San Diego in 1846. That same year, he came back to the city once again on the brig known as *Euphemia*, of which he was one-third owner.

Due to his relationship with the Estudillos, Mr. Davis learned his way around Old Town, San Diego. In 1849, it was Mr. Jose Antonio Estudillo, San Diego's prefect, who pointed out to Davis that the city's original site was unfavorable to its economic growth as a seaport. For the town to prosper, it needed to be relocated near the bay. According to one historian, "San Diego simply could not have come into being with anything like its present position where the Spanish planted the seed of the city in 1769 . . ." (Andrew F. Roll, *William Heath Davis and the Founding of American San Diego*) Andrew B. Gray, chief surveyor for the United States Boundary Commission, came to the conclusion that the waterfront he camped at in the summer months of 1849, was a natural location for a port city. This exact site was in close proximity to the city's harbor, also being accessible to incoming vessels. In February 1850, Mr. Gray discussed this location's appeal with Mr. Davis and suggested that San Diego would indeed grow and prosper if it were relocated near the water's edge. Both men agreed to this proposition, signaling the dawning of "New Town."

By March 1850, William Heath Davis had joined forces with Andrew B. Gray, Jose Antonio Aguirre, Miguel de Pedrorena, and William C. Ferrell for New Town's expansion. Mr. Davis was given the task of constructing a wharf and warehouse within eighteen months. Construction commenced in fall 1850, and was completed by summer of the following year. To construct the wharf and its pier, he was responsible for furnishing and transporting building supplies on his own liners from San Francisco. He once claimed that the wharf cost $60,000. In return, he was to hold on to ownership of the land and its improvements. The business partners received a grant for a tract of 160 acres from the *alcalde* of Old San Diego. Mr. Davis added thirty-two quarter blocks of land to his individual holdings, for which he paid approximately $1,300 or $1,400.

The San Diego Paranormal Research Society heard disembodied vocalizations emanating from the parlor and kitchen areas in the Davis-Horton House. Mr. Davis's daughter, Lillian Davis, has spiritually communicated with the team on many occasions.

It was soon predicted that New Town was in for some good news and prosperous conditions. California was in the Union, and gold in the northern territory ultimately enticed thousands of individuals to the Golden State. Thus, the city was politically and economically changed from a small, quiet pueblo to one of twenty-eight new counties. This new San Diego was one of the first counties to organize and hold elections.

In addition to the wharf, warehouse, and pier, William Heath Davis also erected other buildings, including the William Heath Davis House. This residence became San Diego's premiere frame house—still present today, although it has since been relocated to the city's downtown Gaslamp Quarter. Intriguingly, this saltbox lumber building traveled on the brig *Cybele* around the Horn from Portland, Maine. Its cargo contained 300,000 feet of pine lumber, 40,000 bricks, and around ten completely framed houses. The William Heath Davis House was probably the first permanent structure constructed in New Town, San Diego. It was originally assembled on State Street, between Market and G Streets. Presently it exists at 227 11th Street, between K and L streets.

On December 20, 1968, the *San Diego Union* published an article written by Joe Stone that warned San Diegans that the city's oldest building was going to be torn down to make room for a parking lot. After New Town's eventual demise, most of its buildings were moved to Old Town or utilized as firewood. In 1867, Alonzo E. Horton bought 960 acres adjacent to Davis's New Town. Known as Horton's Addition, this new addition re-established New Town, San Diego.

In 2007, Horton was quoted in a *San Diego Union Tribune* article:

> I found here nothing but a barren waste, with but four straggling buildings, owned by W. Davis, who was the first man to realize the stupendous possibilities of the harbor . . . I bought the few buildings from Mr. Davis and turned one of them into a hotel, the first hotel in San Diego, and placed Captain Dunnells in charge.

The San Diego Hotel was situated on State and F Streets. When people caught on to the historical significance of this 118-year-old house, its owner suggested giving it to the city and subsequently moving it to a different site. In the end, the city chose not to spend the money to relocate the celebrated structure. Its loss made citizens aware of the only other remaining Davis edifice: the William Heath Davis House, now modernly known as the Davis-Horton House. The structure received the addition at the back of the kitchen and a bathroom, as well as having a porch removed. Additionally, it uses gas for cooking and lighting purposes.

In the 1870s, Mrs. Anna Scheper (later known as Mrs. Amos P. Knowles) acquired the house at 227 11th Street. This decision took place just a few days prior to the Board of Supervisors directing her to take control of and board the ill in hospital at a rate of $1.00 per day. From 1872–1882, the "County Hospital" was in the homes of differing private individuals possessing contracts to board and care for ill and impoverished persons.

A late owner, George Deyo, inherited the house in the 1930s and passed it on to the Lanuza Family in 1977, who in turn donated the house to the City of San Diego to become a museum. The house was moved to its current location when the museum restoration began. Electricity was installed for the first time in 1984, and layers of wallpaper were peeled back to reveal earlier décor. Former Museum Curator Mary Joralmon worked tirelessly to restore the house to its current state as a museum for visitors to enjoy.

This little yellow house is known in modern times as the home of the Gaslamp Quarter Historical Foundation (GQHF) and the Gaslamp Museum. Intriguingly, a "saltbox structure" is named after the wooden lidded box that once contained salt granules. Boasting California Historical Landmark status, it is also known as one of San Diego's most haunted locations. To date, only a select few paranormal research teams have been permitted to conduct ghost investigations inside its premises. The San Diego Paranormal Research Society is proud to be one of those teams. In total, it has conducted three investigations into the site's spiritual inhabitants and paranormal occurrences. By utilizing various environmental monitoring equipment, as well as photographic and audio devices, the SDPRS has been able to document and experience various ghost-related phenomena.

One of the most intriguing encounters I have ever experienced occurred inside the Davis-Horton House. I talked about this on an episode of *My Ghost Story: Caught on Camera*. As we walked through the front door, in my mind's eye I immediately saw a young girl with long brown hair and piercing brown eyes. She walked toward me and smiled as if she were greeting us. As I proceeded to put down my equipment bags, I happened to notice this historical black-and-white photograph on a wall at the base of the staircase. Completely speechless, I then asked the docent who the little girl was in the picture. She answered me, saying, "Why, that's Mr. William Heath Davis's daughter, Lillian Davis." Goosebumps covered my entire body, as the image of the youthful girl I saw in my mind's eye completely matched the girl in the photograph.

I had no clue that this photograph even existed, or even that Mr. Davis had a daughter at the time. I have pondered whether this child spiritually resides inside the William Heath Davis House. Furthermore, I have always wondered if she chooses to remain at the historic saltbox lumber home as its ethereal caretaker. Whatever the case is, the intuitive impression I had of Lillian will forever be etched in my heart and soul.

For the remainder of that night's paranormal investigation, the other researchers and I made a strong effort to communicate with Lillian. Many times throughout the late evening hours we heard the disembodied vocalizations of a young girl. At one point, when we were situated in the parlor while conducting an electronic voice phenomena session, we all documented hearing the youthful voice of a young female child emanating from the kitchen area, which is known as one of the hot spot locations for paranormal activity in the home. Additionally, we were able to capture an EVP of a youthful girl saying, "Where's my mommy?" Since there are other spirit forms of young child energies known to make appearances in the Davis structure, we cannot be sure that this aforementioned audio piece was the voice of Lillian.

However, the cadence of the "Where's my mommy?" EVP sounded strikingly similar to a later captured Class A electronic voice phenomenon of a young girl communicating with us. Class A audio captures are the clearest and most profound. When the latter-mentioned vocalization was captured, we were again positioned in the parlor area. At one point, we asked Lillian if she would like to communicate with us. What then ensued was perhaps one of the most profound EVPs I have ever heard and captured. When reviewing my audio from the night's research project, I was speechless after I possibly heard Lillian answer our question, saying, "I am trying to talk to you. My name is Lillian." This capture formidably supported my earlier intuitive impression of Lillian, and also suggested that her spirit possessed some form of intelligence, as opposed to being a residual psychic imprint.

Intriguingly, we were also able to capture an anomalous event on video within just a few minutes of documenting the female EVP vocalization of Lillian introducing herself and letting us know she was trying to talk with us. One of our video cameras was positioned on the lower portion of the staircase, looking up toward the upstairs landing and right-side door leading to the children's room. About five minutes or so after hearing the EVP, we noticed that this door opened of its own volition. After reviewing the footage, we went back to the home to conduct some experiments to see if we could replicate the door opening. We confirmed that there were no air-conditioning currents nor open windows that could have caused this phenomenon. Furthermore, the door is extremely heavy, so one has to put a good amount of force against the door to make it move. If it was opened by Lillian's spirit, perhaps she chose that door due to its connection with children.

The Davis-Horton House is filled with spiritual activity. Some of the occurrences are residual imprints from its days gone by and lack the ability to intelligently commune with the living. Along with Lillian, there are other intelligent energies residing in the home. Even though Mr. Davis never lived inside its premises, he has been spotted from time to time. Many people have witnessed the specter of a woman adorned in Victorian attire as well. A man adorned in military clothing has also been seen, most likely alluding to the home's history as a county hospital. One of the downstairs rooms honors the time when the house catered to the ill, many of whom suffered from tuberculosis, known in those days as "Consumption." The spirits of other children have also been experienced in the home. In addition to Lillian, I have heard the disembodied voice of a very young boy.

The Davis-Horton House was not wired for electricity until 1984. Until then, lighting was provided by gas or coal oil lamps. In fact, a 1977 local newspaper reported that some of these lamps would go off and ignite of their own volition. If these incidents were indeed supernatural in origin, perhaps there was enough spiritual power to cause these anomalies. Even in modern time people still discuss accounts of electrical interference.

Two dear friends of mine, who also happen to be gifted intuitives, have been investigating the paranormal for many years. On a different paranormal investigation a few months later, they both sensed other energies in the home. In the upstairs master bedroom, Sharon psychically sensed the spirit of a man by the name of Charles, who was tall, lanky, and pale. He had very dark hair, and was clad in suspenders and a white shirt. Interestingly, she intuitively picked up another male entity adorned in clothing with blue stripes. Her sister, Dawn, also sensed that this individual was balding and from the late 1890s. The psychic consensus was that these two men were somehow interconnected. Perhaps they were two patients at the former county hospital.

Divining (dowsing) rods are useful metaphysical tools when conducting paranormal research. As the night went on, we decided to conduct a short divining rod experiment. At one point, I asked Lillian if she remembered me from the last time I visited the house. The rods then crossed, indicating "yes." I also asked Lillian if she ethereally inhabits the home by choice. Again, the rods crossed for a "yes." As the night carried on, all of us encountered strangeness inside the home.

Each room in the house depicts a period from its history, from its use as a pre-Civil War military officers' barracks, to a county hospital, to a private residence. Various individuals have occupied the home, including Alonzo Horton (considered the "Father of San Diego"), an alleged German spy, and several families. Today, the Davis-Horton House welcomes thousands of visitors annually.

PART VI:
Maritime Museum of San Diego's Most Haunted

Our oceans are a treasure chest full of seamen stories, legends, and lore. The various ships of the Maritime Museum of San Diego continue to share their historical chronicles as they ebb and flow in the calming tides of San Diego Bay. When you visit these vessels, you can instantly tap into what life was like for the people who sailed aboard. You can also visit the museum's internationally renowned maritime library, which houses a plethora of historical resources about various oceangoing ships.

The Maritime Museum of San Diego boasts a superlative collection of historic ships, including steam-powered vessels, sailing ships, and submarines. The specific ones in its collection include the *America*, a B-39 submarine, the *Californian*, the HMS *Surprise*, a PCF 816 Swift Boat, a San Diego harbor pilot boat, the *San Salvador*, the *Star of India*, the steam ferry *Berkeley*, the steam yacht *Medea*, and the USS *Dolphin*.

The museum offers various educational programs and tours for school-aged children and adults. Historical conservation aboard the *Berkeley* ferryboat consists of a library and archives, including documents pertaining to people's lives on the seas. Known as one of the finest maritime museums in the world, San Diego's Maritime Museum collection includes the history of San Diego Bay, the Pacific Ocean, and coastal California. For the purposes of this book, the three ships that will be discussed are the *Berkeley*, the *Star of India*, and the B-39 submarine.

Chapter 16: B-39 Submarine

A part of the Maritime Museum of San Diego, the B-39 submarine rests in the city's harbor.

Both the *Star of India* and the ferryboat *Berkeley* are widely talked about vessels regarding paranormal activity. However, there are other ships in the maritime museum's collection that also have supernatural occurrences. The B-39 submarine is one of those vessels. Before we delve into the potential reasons behind any ghostly energy submerged within its depths, let us first take a look at its historical influences.

Commissioned in the early 1970s, the B-39 was one of the diesel electric submarines the Soviet Navy labeled "Project 641." These particular vessels were classified as "Foxtrot" by NATO, and were much bigger and more dominant adaptations of German World War II era U-boats. Having served on active duty for more than twenty years, B-39 is among the biggest conservative submarines ever constructed. Her duties were to track US and NATO warships throughout the world's seas. Instrumental during the Cold War's extreme moments, Soviet and then Russian Federation navies organized these submarines from the 1950s through the early 1990s. Today, she is moored in San Diego Bay along with her previous opponents.

Constructed at the Sudomekh Shipyards on the outskirts of Leningrad, the B-39's keel was laid out in 1972. Assigned to the Soviet Fleet's headquarters in Vladivostok, the B-39 and other Foxtrots were primarily utilized for surveillance of United States Navy battle groups, as well as electronic inspection. Additionally, the Vladivostok Submarine Squadron was frequently assigned to patrol the Indian Ocean, Arctic Ocean, Sea of Japan, and the Pacific Ocean. The B-39—code name Cobra—was outfitted with all of the modern advances in engines, sonar, radar, and weaponry. Cobra was eventually decommissioned in 1994, putting an end to its twenty-year vocation as a Cold War combatant. Purchased by private businessmen, she traveled to North America, where she moors as a tribute to all courageous submarine crews during the Cold War.

Her crew consisted of fifty-six sailors, ten midshipmen, and twelve officers. Life on board the B-39 was a culmination of dissimilarity. While the surface brought fresh air, cold showers, and an occasional cigarette, inside brought confined spaces, stale air, hot bunks, and cold food. Imagine having seventy-eight men with only two showers and three toilets! Electricity, light, sound, and activity was minimal, and life was strictly controlled around a three-shift roster, permitting four hours of sleep twice daily, as well as four daily hot meals and a shower once or twice every seven days. There were a series of three shifts, each lasting four hours. Thus, each crew member would twice rotate each shift. A regular mission would typically range anywhere from a week to a month.

You would think that the food supplied on these submarines was average. Actually, Russian submarine crews benefited from some of the most delectable food in the Soviet Navy. Onboard meals were prepared in Department 14's galley. The dining schedule reveals that breakfast was served at 7:00 a.m., dinner at midday, supper at 6–7 p.m., and tea at 10 p.m.

The crew entertained themselves while on a mission, as life inside was not always work and no play. Television and movies were made available, as well as a small library of books. When the submarine was stopped for any period of time, crew members would go fishing off the deck. Due to the occasional long lengths of any given mission, the men aboard were encouraged to partake in their hobby of choice. For example, some would construct metal or plastic submarine models, or compile a photographic album including pictures of that specific voyage.

It is said that places and locations that have seen varying amounts of human emotion almost act as a natural charge for spiritual energy. As we know, life on board the B-39 was as systematic as the mission itself. Thus, putting the aforementioned theory to test, is it possible that these methodical schedules and sailing routes produced a somewhat consistent amount of stress and anxiety, enough to attract paranormal energy? Perhaps the combination of human emotion and electrical components were enough to provide an innate foundation for supernatural activity.

Each vessel within the maritime museum is close in proximity to the others, so some of the paranormal activity on one liner may occasionally show itself on others. Some say that ghostly energy is confined to only one place, while others believe it can exist in more than one location. If this theory holds true, then the B-39 may periodically experience specific supernatural activity native to the *Star of India*, *Berkeley*, or any other ship within the maritime museum.

The B-39 submarine sits adjacent to the collection of maritime museum ships. People are more aware of the ghostly occurrences aboard both the *Star of India* and ferryboat *Berkeley*, mainly because paranormal investigations have been conducted more often on these specific liners. In fact, I am not even sure if anyone has ever participated in a paranormal research project aboard the B-39. Just because the B-39's spiritual encounters are not as widely known does not mean that they do not exist.

Just recently, I traveled aboard the legendary Cobra submarine to learn more about its history. It was intriguing to see the overall layout of the submarine, including all of its interwoven sets of mechanical machinery. From the moment you descend inside its core, you become immediately aware of how orderly and challenging life was while aboard.

While I was perusing the submarine's interior sections, I felt that the energy had a general heaviness about it. I began to feel as if many unseen eyes were watching my every move. When all was silent and the historical video was not running, I heard the disembodied and muffled conversations of men. Intriguingly, I recall detecting a slight Russian accent to them as well. Speaking of possible spirit voices, there are other reports of people hearing ghostly chatter while inside the submarine.

It seems as though the alleged paranormal activity aboard the B-39 is residual in nature. Thus, it is similar to a psychic imprint on the environment replaying over and over at certain intervals. If there is a set pattern to the ghostly events aboard the Cobra, then a series of paranormal research projects would help us comprehend the type of occurring activity.

Chapter 17: *Berkeley* Ferryboat

One of the best maritime libraries in the world sits inside the *Berkeley* ferryboat.

The steam ferryboat *Berkeley* was constructed by the well-known San Francisco Union Iron Works in 1898. This shipbuilding company, developed in 1849, was one of the state's substantial industrial businesses. Interestingly, *Berkeley* was the first vessel built on the west coast that could operate via a screw propeller instead of side wheels. Until 1958, the liner served in the San Francisco Bay ferry system. The *Berkeley* is commended for its assistance with refugee evacuations to Oakland after the 1906 San Francisco earthquake. She worked consistently for three days and nights, carrying people from damaged areas. Also a prized vessel of the Maritime Museum of San Diego, the *Berkeley* is California Registered Historical Landmark No. 1031.

When the *Berkeley* was launched, she was the biggest double-ended vessel ever constructed in the nation. Additionally, she was the premiere successful screw-propelled ferryboat on the west coast. Her design allowed her to shuttle back and forth between piers. Interestingly, she moved in a sideways position while on her docking approach, mainly due to her design and passengers moving to her forward end. She was notorious for running into the dock so often that she was nicknamed the "pile-driver's friend."

The *Berkeley's* main deck (car deck) is situated right above her engine room. A restaurant, bar, and men's restroom were located below, as well as crew accommodations. The vessel also included a saloon (also known as passenger) deck, which was originally restricted for female passengers.

There were many reasons why ferryboats were helpful to California communities. They helped to initiate business affairs and further allowed for development of hard-to-reach land in certain urban areas. The *Berkeley's* service in San Francisco was the second-biggest ferry operation in the United States, with New York Harbor having the largest system.

With the advent of San Francisco's bridges, there was soon to be a lack of need for ferryboats. *Berkeley's* service from Oakland to San Francisco and Alameda to San Francisco was soon replaced by automobile routes and connecting bridges. After the Oakland Bay Bridge was finalized in 1936, the *Berkeley* carried passengers from the city to railroad terminals in Oakland. By 1958, ferry operations had officially declined.

By the end of World War II people preferred to travel by airplane. This had a direct affect on the decline of ferryboat usage. However, the Berkeley received technological improvements after the war. In 1947, the Southern Pacific Railroad installed the first radar device on the liner. She was also known as the only vessel to have a ship-to-shore telephone.

Once ferry service officially declined on the San Francisco Bay, the Golden Gate Fishing Company bought the *Berkeley* on January 26, 1959, with the hopes of utilizing her as a fish reduction liner on the Oakland estuary. In August 1961, Luther Conover became the new official owner of the ferryboat. Once in Sausalito, she opened her doors as a trade fair, where she functioned as a gift shop containing maritime paraphernalia.

The Board of Trustees of the Maritime Museum of San Diego started exploring the possibility of having a floating museum, especially after San Diego and Coronado ferry operations ceased in 1969. The board finally reached its decision to purchase the *Berkeley*, known for her fifty-seven-year run on San Francisco's Bay and her fourteen years as a Sausalito waterfront museum and gift shop. On June 3, 1973, the *Berkeley* sailed into B Street Pier, where she received immediate restoration.

Today, she proudly floats in San Diego's Bay, functioning as an exhibition hall, museum library, archives, and artifact collections, as well as a center for administrative duties. She must be remembered for her one hundred years of service and all of the lives she positively affected during her operative days. Once you step aboard the *Berkeley*, you will be immediately entranced by her nostalgic feel, quiet elegance, and historical charm.

The *Berkeley* is also reputed to be one of San Diego's notable haunted ships. It should come as no surprise, considering her historical significance. Since she is moored adjacent to the *Star of India*, perhaps some of India's spiritual energy visits the *Berkeley* from time to time. Of course, there are other prevailing theories as well. It is postulated that some spiritual energy is attracted to places with lots of emotional ties. I wonder if some of the residual anxiety left over on the ferryboat from the 1906 San Francisco earthquake is enough to act as a battery charge for any paranormal activity. Some people say that the supernatural energy on the *Berkeley* rivals that of the *Star of India* and other maritime ships.

In 2012, I had the opportunity, along with other investigators, to conduct two paranormal research projects aboard the *Berkeley*. Both the Friday night and Saturday night investigations were nothing less than interesting. A paranormal investigator from Orange County and I conducted some audio sessions down in the gallery, where we both heard disembodied vocalizations. These voices seemed to occur very close to us, and at one point it felt as if someone whispered in my ear. Additionally, I was touched on my lower back with what seemed like a gentle hand. Upon review of my audio, an EVP of a child was captured seconds after I said, "Oh, something just touched me. Can you tell me your name?" The angelic voice of a child was heard saying, "Hi."

For the following night's project, I joined forces with a local team by the name Pacific Paranormal Investigations and an Orange County-based group. One of the most compelling experiences occurred in the boiler room. All of us collectively gathered inside this once-boiling hot area and conducted an EVP session. About twenty minutes into the experiment, all of us audibly heard a young female child loudly say "Mommy" two consecutive times in a row. Another researcher and I decided to peruse the upstairs decks just to make sure a living child was not on board or in the vicinity of the adjacent parking lot. Since this was after hours at around 2:00 a.m., we did not locate anyone else on the ferryboat, nor did we see anyone outside. Thus, we could not logically explain this rather loud phantom voice. Needless to say, this emotional, disembodied voice was also captured on all of our recording devices and video cameras. What is intriguing is that the vocalization in person sounded high-pitched, just like a youthful child, but it came through rather whispery on our audio and video devices.

This experience left me with these prevailing questions: Who is this child? Is she looking for her mommy? Is she earth-bound or spirit? Does she need help? I am doing my own research into the vessel's history to possibly find out who this child may be. She may be a residual spirit form from the early days when the vessel was in operation. It always tugs on my heart strings when I experience spiritual voices of children, when all I want for them is to find peace and comfort.

People witness apparitional sightings, experience cold spots, and hear disembodied vocalizations aboard this legendary ferryboat. People have seen a man wearing a fedora hat on board the *Berkeley*, but no one really knows his origins. Some people feel it is the spirit of John O. Norbom, who tragically passed away on board in an incendiary explosion that also injured a few others. In fact, this may be whom Theresa Cannizzaro intuitively sensed the same night in 2012, when we were all aboard the liner. Theresa explained to me that she strongly felt the presence of a young man telling the group to go down to the boiler room. In addition to the child saying "mommy," all of us experienced several ghostly events.

The San Diego Paranormal Research Society will be conducting future projects at the *Berkeley*. Perhaps the people of its past want to remain with the ferryboat they so loved and admired. As with other historically significant locations in San Diego, the *Berkeley* continues to share its days past with visitors from all walks of life.

Chapter 18: *Star of India (Euterpe)*

Originally known as the *Euterpe*, the *Star of India* is one of San Diego's most haunted places. A possible apparition is seen standing in the doorway in the mirror's reflection.

Toward the end of the nineteenth century, thousands of souls emigrated from the British Isles to various areas of our planet. People of the Victorian age and British Empire commenced their journey to colonize the world. Surely this was a daring feat, showing courage and devotion to exploring the unknown and finding new land. These people embarked on fragile ships and sailed inhospitable seas, all the while encountering many hardships on the water. Food and water were limited. Seasickness was unrelenting and injuries abundant. Weather was inclement at times. Happily, people saw the birth of new life. Sadly, people also saw the death of fellow comrades. These people must be remembered for having hearts filled with hope and souls full of bravery. It was the *Euterpe*, now known as the *Star of India*, that carried some of these souls to lands anew. Indeed, the *Star of India* is one of the most legendary ships of all time. Currently moored in San Diego's harbor, she belongs to the city's maritime museum.

The *Star of India* is the oldest iron-hulled merchant ship afloat these days. She was constructed on the Isle of Man in Great Britain, and was officially launched on November 14, 1863, as the *Euterpe*. She was designed to mimic other British merchant vessels of the time. During the trans-Pacific trade (1871–1898), she circumnavigated the globe twenty-one times, with two stops in San Francisco in 1873 and 1883. She carried lumber and living souls, with passenger service from England to India.

As with other ships on dangerous waters, the *Star of India* encountered many near-death disasters while sailing the seas: she endured two collisions and an erupting fire in Liverpool; battled gales and inclement weather; and evaded icebergs, a tragic and fatal occurrence that the RMS *Titanic* encountered in 1912. Additionally, during her lumber voyages she nearly capsized in Newcastle, New South Wales. In 1918, during her travels from Alaska in the spring to San Francisco in the fall, she found herself trapped in ice and endured freezing temperatures which ultimately claimed another ship known as the *Abner Coburn*.

In the early days of 1864, she set sail on her maiden voyage from Liverpool, her home port. She encountered her first disaster out of Liverpool as she ran into a Spanish brig, ultimately damaging her fore-rigging (shrouds and ratlines of the fore lower mast). On her voyage to Calcutta, Colombo, and Madras in 1864, she suffered more damage, losing all three of her masts in a hurricane off Madras. Sadly, her captain, William John Storry, passed away from tropical fever on the return sail.

There were other deaths recorded during the *Star of India's* sailing days, including several children. People were not able to receive advanced medical care that is available to us today, so many of them succumbed to conditions that are now commonly treated and cured. Specifically, eight children were lost on the 1873 voyage:

> Five-month-old Richmond Peachy passed away from pulmonary inflammation and seizures on October 23, 1873.
>
> Eleven-year-old Albert Edward Worger passed away from intestinal issues on November 1, 1873.
>
> Two-year-old Kate Worger passed away from Mesenteria on November 9, 1873.
>
> Fourteen-day-old Thomas Batchelor passed away from exhaustion, as he was born prematurely. He died on November 11, 1873.
>
> Sixteen-day-old Stella Batchelor also passed away from exhaustion the same day as her brother.
>
> Eleven-month-old John Wright passed away from intestinal issues on November 15, 1873.

> Two-year-old Anna Thorsen passed away from whooping cough and seizures on November 27, 1873.
>
> Four-hour-old infant "Behuka" passed away from prematurity on December 17, 1873.

The Alaska Packers Association bought the ship for its Alaskan salmon cannery services during 1902 to 1923. This is when she changed names to the *Star of India.* She is the oldest active sailing ship, sailing from her port in San Diego to the Pacific Ocean. Additionally, the State Department of Parks and Recreation, along with the Maritime Museum of San Diego and the Ancient and Honorable Order of E Clampus Vitus, Squibob Chapter, designated this elderly liner a California Registered Historical Landmark (number 1030) on August 8, 1999.

Euterpe's premiere encounters with California in 1873 and 1883, were brief halts in her journey to load cargo for her voyage around Cape Horn and back to England. This cargo is significant, as it differentiates her as the earliest surviving vessel that participated in California's Pacific Rim trade.

John J. Moore purchased several British-constructed liners with the objective that once Hawaii became part of American territory in 1898, foreign ships registered in that state would automatically pass to American registry. This was important, as originally ships built outside America were prohibited from acquiring American registry trade benefits. Once Mr. Moore bought the *Euterpe* from Shaw, Savill & Albion, he sold her and two other British ships to Lincoln Spencer, a Hawaiian citizen. After a few years as a part of the Indian trade, the stately vessel was placed on voyages to New Zealand and Australia. During this particular era she made her twenty-one voyages around the world. She would depart London, Glasgow, or Liverpool with cabin and emigrant passengers, and proceed into the Atlantic by rounding the Cape of Good Hope and crossing the Indian Ocean. On her return sailings she crossed the Pacific, passing Cape Horn, while heading back into the Atlantic to an English port.

From 1898 through 1900, the ship was heavily involved in the lumber trade. Part of the Pacific Colonial Shipping Company of San Francisco, the *Euterpe* officially became an American ship in 1900. Interestingly, to pave way for the loading and unloading of Pacific Northwest lumber into the vessel two large cuts were made in her stern. Her remaining three trans-Pacific voyages were significant, as she carried wood from Washington State to Australia, towed Australian coal to Hawaii, and carried sugar on her return sailing to the West Coast.

The *Euterpe's* next journey took place in 1902, as she made her first voyage from San Francisco to Bristol Bay during her reign with the Alaska Packers Association. Renamed the *Star of India,* she annually repeated this seafaring expedition until 1923. An interesting story prevails as to how she received her new nomenclature. You see, the Packers picked up four glorious vessels from a world-renowned older line known as "Corry's Irish Stars." These Belfast-constructed ships were called the

Star of Bengal, Star of Italy, Star of France, and *Star of Russia*. The *Euterpe* was referred to as the *Star of India* due to her construction for the Indian trade.

In 1923, after the ship's last voyage to Alaska, James Wood Coffroth came to her rescue, ultimately saving her from the scrap yards. He purchased the tired *Star of India* and handed her over to the Zoological Society of San Diego in 1926. Later, the society gave her to the Maritime Museum of San Diego. Noted author and presenter Capt. Alan Villiers sparked interest in having the ship as part of maritime history; thus hopes of restoration turned into a proud fact, and according to a 1959 dry dock survey, it was found that she could indeed be saved. On July 4, 1976, she was re-launched into San Diego Bay and its neighboring Pacific Ocean, a sure testament to those who believed in her maritime legacy.

All ships have a soul that speaks about their historical past to those residing in the present. It is for these reasons why many ships are said to have spiritual energy. Also ghostly activity may be present on the *Star of India* since people passed away from the physical realm while sailing aboard her decks. The San Diego Paranormal Research Society has conducted official research investigations onboard the *Star of India* and has come away with both intriguing personal encounters and captured ghostly evidence.

There are some well-known hauntings correlated with this oldest sailing ship. One spiritual entity aboard the liner is that of teenager John Campbell. In 1884, he was a stowaway who, when discovered, was put to work on the vessel. One day, while attending to the masts, he slipped and tragically fell. Both of his legs were broken, and he passed away three days later after suffering a great deal of pain. Some people have felt a presence near the masts. Perhaps this is John letting you know that he is near, or to warn you of the danger of being on the masts.

Sadly, while setting up our base of operations in the captains' quarters, we captured an EVP of a young man saying, "Help me." Was this a residual capture of John as he was in a lot of pain? We were able to document other EVPs while stationed in the captain's quarters. When addressing any spiritual energy remaining on the liner we captured someone saying, "Hello, hello" in an adamant tone.

The anchor chain locker has a gruesome history. One day, a Chinese crewman was in the chain locker area in the bow of the ship, going about his usual business. The crewmen above him wanted to raise the anchor and started the machinery to complete that task. Sadly, as the chain filled the storage locker, it physically crushed the poor Chinese crewman. Apparently no one could hear his screams due to the loud roar of the machinery.

Personally, I have a very hard time being in this area. I am quite empathic; thus, I am able to tune into what this poor man must have been going through in the moments leading up to his demise. The energy is thick, and cold spots occur. I have talked to some people who have audibly heard disembodied screams, most likely a residual reminder of this man's experience.

Disembodied vocalizations and EVP captures have been documented by many other paranormal researchers. Many investigators hear phantom conversations that are most likely residual imprints from many years ago. One investigator recorded an ethereal male presence sighing as he was in the process of conducting his audio session. In 2011, Theresa Cannizzaro was on the poop deck (yes, it is spelled correctly) with other paranormal examiners when a strong EVP of a male presence was recorded saying the word "foc'sle." Interestingly, at the time of this surprising capture, the group was joking about how one of the members could not sufficiently pronounce the ship term. It seems as though someone unseen corrected them.

There are many claims of hearing disembodied heavy footsteps on the ship. While conducting our experimentation, we witnessed hearing phantom footsteps above us on the poop deck. In 2014, one of my research colleagues was on the liner one night by himself at 8:30 p.m. in the officer's quarters, when he distinctly heard the phantom sounds of footsteps from above. He even went up to the upwards deck just to make sure the sounds did not emanate from an employee or other ship visitor, and of course, no one living was around.

While in the captain's quarters, all of us noticed that one of the lights above the dining room table would sway on a consistent basis while the other lamp stood still. We tried debunking the swaying, but could not come up with a logical reason as to why one lamp moved on a continuous basis. The water was extremely calm that night, and the ship was not shifting enough to cause significant movement. We are not saying that this occurrence was paranormal in origin; however, we could not naturally explain it. If this was an anomalous incident, perhaps it was a residual phenomenon from the ship's sailing days.

The galley (kitchen area) is also a prominent paranormal hot spot on the *Star of India*. While on one of our investigations we held a vigil there, and it was at this time we started smelling the phantom aroma of baking bread. It was so strong that each team member noticed it, and as soon as it came, it vanished. Another interesting encounter we had during our vigil had to do with some of the kitchenware positioned on shelving units. All of us were stationary at the time when one of the pots fell over; thus, no one accidentally touched any of the items. The water was calm, so we ruled out any ship movement as the cause of this incident. To this day it is something we cannot logically explain.

The tween deck and orlop hold area are also known for having supernatural activity. In my opinion, these two decks are the most spiritually active. The SDPRS team has heard disembodied footsteps and a general rustling sound. We also heard the audible vocalizations of a female energy. Shadow figures have been seen roaming about various decks. In fact, Theresa Cannizzaro shared with me an interesting experience she had one night while investigating the tween deck with a few other colleagues. She relayed that she saw a white shadow manifest into human form, which seemed to de-materialize and materialize for about a minute. To prevent any sort of light coming in from the outside they made sure the portholes were covered with tin foil.

One night, as we were conducting a lengthy EVP session on the aft end of tween deck, a solidly black humanoid shadow figure emerged and quickly moved across

A close-up of the possible apparition seen in the doorway to the captain's quarters. While conducting paranormal research, SDPRS Co-Director Ali Schreiber saw a fast-moving ghostly specter in the exact location of this photograph.

a portion of the deck. We had one of our infrared cameras pointing in the direction of the anomaly, but it was not recorded. It has been said by some intuitively inclined individuals that an angry ethereal being makes itself known in the orlop hold. I have investigated this area many times and I have not once experienced any gruff energy.

One of the highlight experiences we had actually occurred in this lower deck. During our audio session we heard a chair slide across the floor. We spent considerable amounts of time trying to explain the noise. When we came upon a chair and moved it, the sound of its movement matched what we heard moments before. There was no rhyme or reason as to why this piece of furniture moved of its own volition. Along with other researchers, Theresa shared with me another fascinating experience she had, which eerily echoes the aforementioned occurrence. She described hearing the loud sound of what seemed like a large piece of metal being dragged across the floor in the foc'sle. Showing responsibility as investigators, Theresa and her teammates made sure that no other living person was on the ship at the time of this encounter. No one else living was present.

PART VII:
North County San Diego's Most Haunted

Chapter 19: AVO Playhouse

In the heart of Vista, California, the AVO Playhouse is full of spirited energy.

History reigns among the rolling hills and trees of North County San Diego. Its topography is etched with a storied past, and many of its historic edifices blend their times gone by with the present. I have a special place in my heart for this area of the county, as it houses the Rancho Buena Vista Adobe, where my team has been conducting its own private paranormal research in addition to its monthly fundraising "Spirits of the Adobe" tours for over seven years. Surely the sites mentioned in this section are among the most widely discussed in terms of history and ghostly happenings.

Opened on December 11, 1948, the AVO Playhouse was constructed by S. Charles Lee using geodesic dome methods as a single-screen theater with about 800 seats. Located at 303 Main Street in Vista, California, the AVO was the second movie house in town and four times the size of the Vista Theatre, its main competitive rival. Abe Shelhoup was the proprietor, and Clell E. McElroy was the manager, along with his partner Joseph H. Fotheringham, Vista's first mayor. Electricity was provided by Bice Electric. B. F. Shearer Company was responsible for providing the furnishings. W. W. Allen supplied the decorations and paints. It was named in honor of Vista's nickname, "The Avocado Capital of the World." Its lobby was designed to replicate the shape of an avocado.

The playhouse had an 18 ft. × 24 ft. screen at a construction cost of $100,000. In addition to movies, it was the home of the Miss Vista contest and theater musicals. With 140 lodges in the back, the cost to see a movie was a mere ninety cents. On opening day at 6:45 p.m., *A Night Has a 1,000 Eyes*, starring Edward Robinson, proudly played on its screens. Prior to the actual movie patrons saw a cartoon and newsreel.

It closed its doors on May 29, 1989, due to the arrival of cinematic multiplexes. With support from "Friends of the AVO," the City of Vista's Moonlight Stage Productions revived and renovated the building in 1994. It was then opened as the AVO Playhouse in 1995, as the home of the Winter Moonlights. Although the exterior and lobby area still exist as first constructed, the auditorium has been stripped of any original decorations, including the removal of the proscenium opening. The AVO Playhouse continues showing small town community theater productions.

Today, the AVO Playhouse is known as one of Vista's haunted gems. Many theaters are known to have paranormal activity. Think about the scores of emotions that take place inside their confines. The marketing specialist for the City of Vista asked the San Diego Paranormal Research Society to conduct a thorough investigation of the AVO Playhouse July 20, 2013, through July 21, 2013, as many people have had odd experiences while inside the playhouse. While conducting eye-witness interviews this employee went on to say:

> In October, we were producing a performance at the AVO. It was a Tuesday night. I was sitting toward the back of the house on the right side. During the show I looked up to the balcony. I saw a man in a white long-sleeved shirt and khaki colored pants standing next to the follow spot. I was actually producing this event, and knew of nobody who would be up in that area, except for the light board operator in the booth adjacent to the follow spot. The man stood there for a few seconds, looking at the stage while the show was going on, then turned and seemed to glide away. As with other experiences I have had before, I had a buzzing feeling in my head which ended after he disappeared. Personally, I feel it could have been the spirit of the former owner of the AVO, who ran it for decades. I have to get his name—I believe his first name was Willy, but I will confirm it. Anyone who grew up in Vista remembers him from when he ran the AVO as a movie theater. In high school, when I would go to a movie at the AVO, he would be there.

Other individuals have spotted this male spirit form as well. While conducting the investigation, a couple SDPRS members mentioned that they, too, saw a man dressed in a similar style of clothing. A team member showed a historical photograph of the former theater manager, Mr. Willis, to the employee that accompanied us on our research project. When he looked at the picture, he told us that the apparition he saw was definitely that of Mr. Willis.

While talking to the assistant technical theater coordinator about his experiences, he went on to say:

> I've had a few experiences in the AVO. I've felt the sense of being watched there often. From the stage, I'll sometimes think that I see movement in the upstairs booth area. The upstairs hallway has an uneasy feeling to it and a cold spot just upstairs to the right of the first doorway (under the blue ceiling light). I generally feel like someone is behind me at all times in that hallway, and quite often the hair on the back of my neck will stand up when I'm up there. I've heard creaking upstairs while down in the lobby that sounds somewhat like movement in the hallway.
>
> Two years ago, in March or May, we were building the set for Foxfire and I was alone on stage while my supervisor went out for supplies. The stage left [your left as you look out into the audience] side of the set was a rustic log cabin with a front porch and screen door. I was working backstage left inside of the cabin when I heard my supervisor step up on to the cabin's porch (it was quite creaky when walked upon). I looked out in front of the cabin from the stage left wing and didn't see him, so I went through the cabin and out on to the porch to meet him and found the stage empty and cold.
>
> The hair on my neck stood straight up. There was no doubt in my mind that someone (presumably my supervisor) had walked up on stage and on to the porch. I didn't think that the noise sounded out of place or odd at all and fully expected to see him there with my needed supplies. It took a moment to realize that I was still alone in the building and I very quickly became uneasy. I left the stage and went to the lobby until he returned. I did not see anything on stage that day, but it certainly felt like someone was there.

Cleaning crews have also encountered high strangeness inside the AVO's confines. They have reported that they heard the disembodied laughter of a man on the upstairs balcony on more than one occasion. Could this be Mr. Willis still looking after the theater? Most recently, our SDPRS Vista historical consultant shared that another cleaning crew staff member saw an apparition sitting in the seating areas and terminated her employment soon thereafter.

Interestingly, the apparition of a male farmer has been spotted in the audience section of the theater. Since Vista, California, was fertile farming land many years ago, this sighting is not all that surprising. On the investigation at the AVO a *San Diego Union Tribune* reporter joined the SDPRS crew as they conducted its research project. As the reporter was interviewing me about the team and what our plans were for the night, I noticed this tall man wearing farming clothes and a long vintage brown coat. When I glanced over and saw him he appeared slightly translucent, standing in the stage left seating area around row F. To date, it is one of the best apparitional sightings that I ever had and is described in the article "Stories Spark Ghostly Probe at AVO: Paranormal Researchers Investigate AVO Playhouse," available online at http://www.sandiegouniontribune.com.

We spent a considerable amount of time in the upstairs hallway leading to the projection booth area and the balconies. We were told that many people get uneasy feelings while walking through the upstairs corridor. In one of the storage rooms adjacent to the projection booth area, we found that the air conditioning and heating unit emitted high amounts of EMF (electromagnetic field). Some people react to elevated EMF levels and experience anxiety, paranoia, flu-like symptoms, etc. Thus, we feel peoples' reports of uneasiness while upstairs could be attributed to the significant EMF readings in that area. Are the spiritual energies also utilizing the EMF as a battery and energy source? Yes, it is very possible, as this could explain the visual sightings and disembodied voices common to the area.

It seems as though the environment was in our favor the night of our debut investigation of the playhouse. A full moon was in store for July 21. This is quite interesting, as a full moon is theorized to manipulate spiritual energy. The same goes for magnetic disturbances and geomagnetic storms. A minor disturbance took place on July 21, with a G1 geomagnetic storm expected on July 26.

Each SDPRS member had unique personal experiences during the investigation. We also felt some extreme cold spots, noticed shadowy, humanoid figures out of our peripheral vision, and heard disembodied voices from days past. Would these experiences have occurred if the moon phase and/or magnetic fluctuations were not present? Maybe or maybe not. That is the beauty of paranormal research: putting the puzzle pieces together and finding correlations to anomalous activity.

Speaking of personal experiences, I had similar intuitive impressions of a little girl around ten or eleven years old. As we were all seated on the stage during an EVP session, we heard the disembodied voice of a small female child throughout the night. One of our members strongly sensed that the girl's name was Natalie. She also picked up that this young ethereal energy had stage fright in her mortal years. So far, we have not found any records indicating that this little girl had any direct connection to the AVO Playhouse.

Sandra Ellis-Troy was a former actress during the AVO's heyday, capturing the hearts of many with her memorable performances. Troy was well-known in North County's theater circle and adept at playing vibrant female characters. One of her unforgettable acts was her astounding depiction of an Alzheimer's patient in the New Village Arts' production of *The Waverly Gallery* in 2005, at the AVO Playhouse. She passed away in December 2010. Many people attribute their ghostly encounters to Mrs. Troy. She touched the lives of many throughout her life and quite possibly continues her legacy in spirited form.

One of the assistant technical directors had a unique experience that could very well be linked to Mrs. Troy, especially since she was to star in the show that they were preparing for, but she had passed away a few months prior. This employee was working by himself in the middle of the day on the very set that Sandra was scheduled to appear in. While going along with his business, he heard the building's front doors open up to the sound of someone walking down the aisle and up on the stage. When he looked around, he did not see any living person in the facility. With nerves running high, he waited to go back to work until someone else showed up.

Some of our audio captures may correlate to Mrs. Troy as well. We captured a faint EVP of "yeah" after we asked Mrs. Troy if she worked at the theater with Mr. Willis. A few minutes later I asked the question, "Do you work here?" I audibly heard a female voice answer my question, but I was not able to decipher what was said.

Our second research project at the AVO occurred on September 12, 2015. The night of this investigation we had a chance for thunderstorms. It is theorized that lightning can increase paranormal activity with its atmospheric electrical charges. If ghosts and/or spirits are made of electricity, then it is safe to say that they utilize ionic energy during thunderstorms to manifest and gain energy.

We spent a considerable amount of time in the upstairs projection area. All of us experienced hearing the faint sound of anomalous voices. Again, I heard the identical-sounding vocalization of a young female child. Activity started to pick up when one of the team members shared her theater experiences from Grossmont College. In fact, I heard a disembodied female ask, "Can you invite me?" when the team member was talking about the plays she participated in while at college. About twenty-seven minutes into our session, I started to feel quite drained. This could have been due to the high EMF. We then felt the temperature drop and a few seconds later heard disembodied whispers.

Utilizing the Singapore Theory, one of the teammates experimented by "running a show." Singapore Theory is used in paranormal research as a means of creating a familiar environment of a particular time period. It was during this experiment when I had the second profound apparitional sighting at the AVO. While videotaping the seating areas from up above in the balcony, I saw a figure wearing a dress walk down the aisle and dissipate right in front of my eyes. Unfortunately, my camera was surveying the seats in closer proximity from the stage, so I was not able to document it. A few minutes prior to this visual encounter, I noticed someone sitting in the seats on stage right. Interestingly, at the same time I saw this specter another teammate documented hearing someone sit down in the exact same vicinity.

Later on in the investigation we decided to spend some time in the dressing rooms. A lot of people hear disembodied voices in this area, so we decided to run some tests. There is an outside alleyway behind the backstage area; thus, we discovered that the sound of people talking while outside can definitely infiltrate the dressing room area, even as far as the stage and first few rows of seating.

We conducted a brief dowsing rod experiment inside the dressing rooms. We indicated the rods to cross for YES answers and separate for NO answers. Toward the end of the session I felt completely tired and drained. Of course, this could be due to the hot and humid temperature in San Diego at the time. The results of this dowsing rod experiment are as follows:

Rods crossed YES when we asked the spirits to let us know of their presence.

Rods crossed YES when we asked if anyone participated in plays at the AVO. We then asked the rods to uncross, and they did.

Rods crossed YES when we asked if anyone helped out with the theater's technology.

Rods crossed YES when we asked if anyone spent time up in the projection booth. It was at this time that we heard a possible response to the question.

Rods crossed YES when we asked if there was a male spirit with us. At this time we heard footsteps and I encountered a cold spot.

Rods crossed YES when we asked if he or she was an actor or actress.

Rods crossed YES when we asked if anyone used the dressing rooms.

Rods crossed YES when we later asked if there was a female spirit with us.

Rods crossed YES when we asked if she performed at the AVO.

Rods crossed YES when we asked if there were more than two energies with us.

Utilizing metaphysical tools is helpful during investigations, but as with other tools and gadgets, the results do not really prove anything, as the paranormal is not an exact science. With this said, certain results do indicate the possible presence of paranormal activity. It is safe to say that the rods' movements correlate to some of the AVO's history and spiritual activity.

Upon finishing our investigations, we came to an agreement that the AVO Playhouse has a plethora of spiritual activity from various time periods. Both residual and intelligent energies seem to exist at the historic theater, with a mixture from its farming and entertainment days. As we exited the playhouse, we decided that a third investigation was warranted—more or less to further connect the pieces of the theater's paranormal puzzle.

Chapter 20: Elfin Forest

San Diego is known for its abundance of natural resources. Offering close to eleven miles of recreational opportunities such as hiking, mountain biking, equestrian trails, and scenic lookout points, Elfin Forest Recreational Reserve is a 784-acre area developed by OMWD in partnership with the San Diego County Water Authority and the US Department of Interior: Bureau of Land Management.

Premiering in 1992, this geographical location has been planned to combine the intrigue of domestic water supply development, natural resources management, and recreational activities. Its innate attractiveness consists of native plant varieties (such as oak riparian, oak woodland, coastal sage shrub, and chaparral) and many types of wildlife indigenous to the region.

This popular location also provides many opportunities for educational research and environmental appreciation. Furthermore, it is situated within the Escondido Creek watershed, flowing from Lake Wohlford to San Elijo Lagoon all year long. Additionally, the reserve displays six selected overlooks including picnic tables and magnificent views of the Pacific Ocean, Channel and Coronado Islands, the Laguna and San Bernardino mountains, and the Olivenhain Dam and reservoir. For adventure seekers, the recreational reserve's park rangers offer guided group tours and student educational programs designed to promote environmental awareness and preservation methods.

North County's Harmony Grove Spiritualist Fellowship and Questhaven Retreat Center is within Elfin Forest. Founded by Rev. Flower A. Newhouse and her husband, Lawrence Newhouse, the Christward Ministry at Questhaven Retreat is a sacred setting that allows worshippers from all over the world to study and be closer to God. Newhouse was born with the intuitive gift of clairvoyance and has spent many years re-awakening humanity to the reality of angelic life.

On August 4, 1940, during the dedication service inside Oak Grove Sanctuary, Mrs. Newhouse uttered the following words: "And now in the awareness of what we do, we reverently bequeath Quest Haven to the Christ, forever." The retreat facility is a non-denominational Christian training facility devoted to revealing unity in various faiths. Miles of meditation sites and natural trails were added. It has long been thought that people can be drawn closer to the Almighty when set deep within nature and the wilderness. Today, the 655-acre retreat continues the legacy of Mr. and Mrs. Newhouse. Nowadays, budding residential communities and bustling commercial businesses have infiltrated the area. Many years ago, the land was barren except for animal life, dense foliage, and possible sites of Native American villages.

Chapter 20: Elfin Forest

The Elfin Forest Recreational Reserve is rumored to be supernaturally active. Legend suggests that gypsies and their social relatives once resided in the area at the turn of the nineteenth century and into the twentieth century. A portion of this fable postulates that natives from adjacent neighborhoods penetrated the location and coerced the gypsies off the land, murdering those who resisted. The unrealistic anecdote to this myth suggests that the gypsies in turn cursed the Elfin Forest and its adjoining communities. Some say it was this exact curse that initiated the various supernatural occurrences. Not surprisingly, this entire legend has not been confirmed. In all, the genesis of this elaborate tale was most likely derived from an overactive creative mind.

Other mythic fables abound for Elfin Forest, so it comes as no surprise that a preconceived notion of otherworldly phenomena develops in the subconscious. One of the outrageous claims has to do with a ten-foot white owl that rules the skies above as it seeks out unsuspecting people on the mysterious grounds below. A tad bit more absurd is the legend of a witch riding her phantom black stallion. Apparently, this female wraith-like figure possesses a keen vision for detecting trespassers. Some people associate the Questhaven Retreat Center, erected in the 1940s, as the former site of an insane asylum—another legend that has not been verified by fact. Obviously, these are all overdone, make believe tales with the ultimate intent to create humor and fear at the same time.

One of the prevailing ghostly legends has to do with an apparition known as the Lady in White. Her presence has been witnessed since the 1940s. One explanation for her origin suggests that she was the wife of a regional settler who happened to be perusing the forest for her lost children, thus undeniably paralleling the Mexican folklore legend of La Llorona. She is occasionally seen adorned in a veil and long dress. Observers have witnessed her spiritual form independently roaming the forest's wilderness and also near the Escondido Creek's banks.

In *San Diego Specters*, author John Lamb describes possible natural explanations for the area's rumored ghostly activity. You see, since the 1960s, Elfin Forest has seen its share of teenage parties, alcoholic drinking fests, and suspected occult rituals, leading to altered awareness caused by the ingestion of alcohol, which could possibly lead to overactive imaginations and/or hallucinations. Furthermore, could some people's alleged ghostly encounters be the product of intended teenage pranks on unsuspecting visitors? Mr. Lamb also mentions the possibility of misconstruing roaming wildlife for ghosts and spirits. Additionally, occasional fog moves into the area and swirls around, thus leading to false positive sightings of paranormal activity.

I have talked with a few people who have felt the feeling of being watched by unseen eyes while visiting the Elfin Forest. A few years ago I went on a moderate-level hike with one of my friends. At certain points on the hike, I felt the distinct feeling that someone was watching my every move. Simultaneous to these sensations, I also felt anxiety and panic that were not my own. The experience was so intense that I had to leave the area, as I felt a sense of impending doom. Once I left the location these sensations went away. Award-winning author Marie Jones shares a similar intriguing experience she had while driving through the area:

I cannot truly say I've ever encountered an actual ghost or apparition, but I can say I've experienced places where the energy felt as though someone turned down the vibrational dial from 10 to 1; places that felt so "negative," even foreboding, that I felt compelled to get out as soon as possible.

The first occasion was when I was about fourteen. My family had just relocated from New York to San Diego, so of course a trip to the Hotel del Coronado was in order. I'd never heard at the time of the hotel's long, rich haunted history. We were on a tour of the hotel and I noticed a hallway that was roped off. My mom or dad asked about it and we were told it was off limits due to renovations. But I got such a feeling of intense dread when I moved toward that area my stomach lurched. I recoiled, moving off with my family. Later, I learned that particular part of the hotel was allegedly haunted and it all made sense. I had picked up on the negative energy present. I realized then I was somewhat empathic and could detect energy shifts easily.

About three years later, my boyfriend and I went to a Halloween party at a big mansion in La Jolla, a gorgeous and affluent seaside town. I don't remember the street the house was on, but it was an old house, and everyone was told not to go into a particular room to put down our coats and purses. We just thought it was because the homeowners didn't want partiers in that room . . . but later in the evening I wasn't paying attention and accidentally went into the room, thinking it was where I left my purse. I was literally pushed backwards by some unseen force with a sense of absolute dread. It felt as though hands were upon me, pushing me out of the room and back into the hall. Again, my stomach lurched and I almost vomited.

Because I was too embarrassed about having mistakenly gone into the room we were all told to stay out of, I never said a word. Only later, when friends were talking about how fun the party was, did I learn that the forbidden room was said to be haunted from a murder that had taken place in the house decades earlier! I saw nothing—no ghosts or apparitions while in the room. But I felt something that was not normal, something so strong it made me turn tail and run.

The third situation occurred in North County, namely in the Questhaven area near where I live now in San Marcos. At the time I was in my twenties, and the area was mostly uninhabited open space with lots of woods and a few horse properties peppered here and there. I had heard of the local legend of the Lady in White that roamed the area called Elfin Forest, and for some reason just decided one day to go and see what the fuss was all about.

I refused to drive into the area alone at night, so I went during broad daylight, on a typical sunny San Diego day. Not a cloud in the sky, because you know it never rains in Southern California. I drove down what was at the time Questhaven Road (it is now almost fully built up with homes and sadly more coming), and I was all alone on the dirt road, surrounded by trees on either side. I was enjoying the scenery as I moved into the Elfin Forest area. The local legend stated the Lady haunted the area near the Christian mystical retreat on top of the hill known as Questhaven, which was at the end of a winding dirt road that led up to a large iron double gate.

I never even made it that far when the skies suddenly turned a very ominous dark grey, so much so it looked like twilight, although my watch confirmed it was early afternoon. It began raining, no, *pouring*, and I started to panic a little. Here I was on a dirt road to nowhere, looking for a ghost, and the sunny skies had just shifted so fast it made my head spin. Determined to keep going, I drove forward slowly until I reached a point in the road where a fallen tree blocked my way. I needed to turn around, and an arising sense of terror was making it hard to focus. I tried turning my car around but had little room to maneuver. As my panic rose, the rains fell harder and the road began flooding. I somehow managed to inch my car completely around and tore down the dirt road back home as quickly as I could.

When I got to the main road leading back into suburban San Marcos the skies were clear and sunny again! Not only that, but the streets were bone dry, yet my car was dripping with rainwater!

I don't know what happened that day, or if it had anything to do with the Lady in White at all, but I've never forgotten that feeling of pure terror and tightness in my chest. That road is now paved, and I've been down it many times lately—even gone to hike a few times up at Questhaven, and could never quite identify the place this happened (I experienced absolutely nothing out of the ordinary on more recent trips!). I'm sure it has drastically changed with time. But I do still have the occasional sense of foreboding driving in the area, and I do still have nightmares of being trapped on a flooded dirt road in the middle of nowhere, with rain pouring down on my car, sure that the Lady in White is hiding in the trees watching me with a wicked smile.

I now try to avoid any place I get an immediate sense of negative energy in, despite my curiosity to find out why. Some things are better left unknown!

Is the Elfin Forest Recreational Reserve really inhabited by ghosts and spirits? With so many probable, logical explanations at the forefront, it lessens the veracity of genuine supernatural events. However, could there be intermittent ghostly activities here, especially considering the rich historical events common to San Diego and other Southern California locations? Perhaps there are residual psychic imprints left over from when Native Americans roamed the regional areas. Research documents the existence of Northern Diegueño Indian tribes occupying the land

9,000 years ago. Did the influences of Mr. and Mrs. Newhouse somehow pave the way for a foundation of spiritual activity through the years? Perhaps the entire location is spiritually and intuitively charged from the studies and teachings at Questhaven Retreat Center. Regardless of any spiritual phenomena, Elfin Forest is an inherently beautiful part of San Diego's North County region.

Chapter 21: Escondido Public Library

Mexico gained its freedom from Spain in 1821, and various lands were developed into ranchos and handed over to prominent California Mexicans in 1834. Juan Bautista Alvarado, a native San Diegan, received the land grant in the Escondido territory known as El Rincon del Diablo, where he established a residence and raised cattle. Once Alvarado and his wife passed away, their children sold their portions of the rancho to a local judge named Oliver S. Witherby.

Once he obtained entire portions of his terrain, Mr. Witherby started farming significantly and increased the population of his cattle and sheep herds. Intriguingly, he also commenced gold mining on his property in the early 1860s. Additionally, he constructed a mill to grind ore and officially named it the Rincon del Diablo and Escondido Mining Company. The title of his mill held the first utilization of the word "Escondido," meaning "hidden" in Spanish language.

The ensuing years brought along other plans for the Escondido area. In 1868, due to financial limitations, Mr. Witherby sold his land to Edward McGeary and the three Wolfskill brothers. They augmented the ranch to primarily raise sheep, so for several years, a portion of the Escondido valley was referred to as Wolfskill Plains. In 1883, some men developed the Stockton Company, having purchased the rancho for $128,138. A vineyard was then established consisting of Muscat grapes. On March 1, 1886, the Escondido Company transferred the terrain to the Escondido Land & Town Company for a little over $100,000. Its main purpose was to subdivide the land and establish more citrus groves and vineyards. When land development expanded in the 1950s, many of the eastern vineyards became private residence sites. In 1886, various wells were drilled to supply irrigation water to the numerous groves.

Often labeled the "Hidden Valley," the City of Escondido was incorporated on October 8, 1888, with a populace of 249. Running north and south, the town site streets were named in honor of various indigenous trees and plants. Running east and west the avenues were named after states. The town's main shopping thoroughfare was called Grand Avenue. Today, Escondido is known as one of North County's most attractive areas to live.

The Escondido Public Library is a nicely sized building in the heart of Escondido, just a ways down the street from the old hospital. The structure commenced its service to Escondido in 1894, as a private facility situated in the small building in Grape Day Park. In 1898, the City of Escondido took over all operations, establishing it as a city-funded department. In 1910, the new library was constructed on Kalmia and Third Avenue with the aid of Andrew Carnegie funds and a land contribution.

In 1980, Escondido expanded to a population of 67,000. Thus, plans were underway to set aside space for a new facility. In December 1980, the library was relocated to the modern-day, two-story, 40,000-square-foot site. In 1996, the Pioneer Room opened its doors with the help of local historian Frances Beven Ryan. Four years later, the computer center was integrated in the Pioneer Room due to a grant from the Bill & Melinda Gates Foundation. Renovations including air conditioning, elevators, carpeting, and added space took place in 2010.

Ali Schreiber and I were honored to be asked to conduct a paranormal research project at the Escondido Public Library in August 2016. The site has many interesting claims of supernatural activity directly witnessed and experienced by several library staff. According to Viktor, the senior librarian in adult services, there have been a few apparitional sightings, mainly in the downstairs stacks and seating areas. A male specter has also been spotted in the downstairs lobby.

Additionally, there are reports of the staff elevator going up and down when no one is inside the building. Technical examination reveals proper functioning; thus, there is no obvious logical explanation for it running of its own volition. Disembodied vocalizations are heard throughout the building, as well as the sounds of books being removed and placed on the shelving units. One of the security guards has heard footsteps upstairs while he is alone in the building at night.

On the night of our official research project, we met up with the senior librarian at the location for a walk through and staff member interviews. It also gave us a chance to map out the course of our investigation and determine how much time we wanted to devote to each individual area. After the preliminary, we came to the consensus that the alleged paranormal activity at the site was a mixture of residual and intelligent. Based on various employee accounts, we decided to primarily conduct audio, photographic, and videographic experiments throughout the night.

Ali and I discussed the various theories for the ethereal phenomena occurring at the Escondido Public Library. Of course, the history of the area most likely serves as a foundation for the ghostly encounters in the building. Additionally, the edifice is situated right between the old hospital and the neighboring crematorium, perhaps adding an extra layer of spiritual energy. Constant human traffic may also increase paranormal activity, in addition to the energy attached to each individual book. Each book has been checked out many times, having gone to various residences throughout Escondido. Even with all of these prevailing theories, there are perhaps elusive reasons for the supernatural energy occurring at this library.

We commenced our investigation upstairs in the children's area and spent a considerable amount of time conducting both a vigil and audio experiments. One of the major claims in this space is the sound of disembodied footsteps when no one is inside. I had a profound experience upon entering the area during our initial walkthrough, a particular encounter I have only experienced once before while aboard the legendary RMS *Queen Mary* in Long Beach, California. About three seconds after walking inside this area I momentarily felt disoriented, almost like vertigo, and felt some sort of energy go right through me.

While conducting an extensive EVP session in the area, I noticed a humanoid shadow form manifest near the southwest corner where the computers are located.

Intriguingly, this sighting occurred shortly after a unique EVP capture. I asked, "Are you connected to the library at all or the land?" Upon review of my audio, I heard a male response "yes" right after I said the word "library." Interestingly, this vocalization was not captured on my other TASCAM® audio recorder.

Theory postulates that places with high amounts of EMF may serve as capacitors for spiritual energy. We put this hypothesis to the test while examining the claims in one of the upstairs offices. An electrical utility room sits just adjacent to this specific space; thus, could the generated EMF serve as a natural conductor for the ghostly occurrences in this office? Could it be charging the entire upstairs portion of the library?

According to the senior librarian, the staff member assigned to this particular office has documented strange activity, mainly the sound of someone typing on the computer keyboard when no one is present. While we were inside, I decided to type on the keyboard to compare the sound to what was previously heard. While doing this, we happened to capture a surprising EVP; upon review of the audio, we heard a female voice almost intelligently say, "There you go" while I was typing.

As the night progressed, we also spent a considerable amount of time in the upstairs event space known as the Turrentine Room. Upon entering the room, I felt that the energy had a general heaviness or thickness. We decided to run some Instrumental Trans Communication experimentation in addition to a general EVP session. I heard an audible answer "yes" to the question "Were you here before the library was built?" We also heard a male response "yes" after Ali asked, "If there is anyone here, can you say hello?" A female vocalization of "Hi" directly followed thereafter.

Furthermore, the name "William" came through our spirit box after Ali asked, "Can you use this device to tell us your name?" Does the name historically refer to one of the organizers of the Escondido Land & Town Company, whose name was William Thomas? Other managers included President Jacob Gruendyke, as well as four other Kansas-based Thomas brothers and business colleagues.

After debriefing in the senior librarian's office, we had to walk through a series of other cubicles before exiting back out to the lobby area. As we were passing through I noticed one of the books I wrote and donated to the library. Ali mentioned how I should sign my book, and upon audio review, we captured an EVP of a woman saying "good times" right after we finished talking.

Staying downstairs for the remainder of the night, we had some interesting experiences while situated within the stacks near the teenage section. As mentioned, a library employee has described hearing books being placed and removed off the shelves when closing up for the night. Another staff member shared with us while alone downstairs she had seen ghostly figures moving in between the different rows of stacks.

Throughout the night Ali and I felt cold spots, as well as having occasional shadow figure sightings. We examined the shadows produced by the reflections of car headlights, as we wanted to make sure that they were not being mistaken for authentic paranormal sightings. However, the couple manifestations we witnessed represented humanoid forms. Furthermore, Ali documented hearing what sounded like someone running their fingers across the books; thus, she went ahead and attempted to match the sound by doing it herself. The sounds completely coincided with each other. Throughout our experimentation, we also heard what sounded like furniture being moved. At one point the senior librarian heard a female humming as well.

Perhaps the strangest incident occurred toward the end of our investigation while we were downstairs. We are not sure if the experience indicates residual or intelligent spiritual activity. Here is the transcript of our recording:

Ali: "Do you want to try a spirit box session?"

Nicole: "Yeah, I was just thinking that. [Talking to Viktor] She read my mind. We tried this upstairs, but there was a Spanish station that kept coming through."

Viktor: "Yeah"

Ali: "Do you mind if I have some of your water?"

Nicole: "No, not at all."

EVP: A male vocalization of "lose my mind" occurs right after.

People have also seen a female apparition adorned in a light-colored dress move around the various downstairs stacks. Even though we did not directly see the ethereal entity, we did capture an intriguing spirit box recording that may correlate with the sighting. At one point I asked, "Who is the woman who is wearing the white dress?" Almost immediately a female voice emanated through the box saying what sounds like "me."

After our research project and the review of our results, we do agree that there is some sort of paranormal energy at the Escondido Public Library. The energy seems pleasant and curious, and more related to the history of the land as opposed to the location itself. We did find out that a homeless individual passed away on one of the corners near the library. He used to be a regular patron of the library; perhaps he continues to visit the premises in the spiritual realm. Even with proposed theories attempting to explicate the reasons behind supernatural activity, there is still a dose of obscurity that makes the paranormal so elusive. Ali and I are quite honored to have been asked to conduct an official investigation into the library's mysterious claims.

Chapter 22: Rancho Guajome

Rancho Guajome was a 2,219.41-acre land grant about halfway between Vista and Bonsall. It was titled after the Luiseño Indian village wakhavumi, or "place of the frogs." It originated from the San Luis Rey grazing lands after secularization was officiated by Governor Jose Figueroa in 1834. Like the RBVA, it is one of the very few remaining land ranchos where cattle and sheep roamed and grazed the nearby hills. The stunning property lies three miles northwest of Vista and six miles east of Oceanside.

On July 19, 1845, Governor Pio Pico issued the land to mission Indians Andres and Jose Manuel. According to the 1860 census, there were eighteen Luiseño peoples at the Guajome and 118 at Mission San Luis Rey's Luiseño village. In fact, Mission San Luis Rey, founded in 1798, became the biggest mission, with nearly 3,000 residents during the 1820s. These native people were hunters and gatherers; their food supplies consisted of wild game, reptiles, insects, and sea life from the Pacific Ocean.

Affluent landowner and businessman Abel Stearns purchased the sprawling rancho for $550. Stearns married San Diego's political and social leader Don Juan Bandini's daughter, Dona Arcadia. Col. Cave Johnson Couts married Dona's sister, Ysidora Bandini, on April 5, 1851. Rancho Guajome was handed over by Stearns to the bride and groom as a substantial wedding gift. They resided in Old Town until 1853, when they relocated north to Rancho Guajome with their two San Diego-born children. The couple had eight more children who were born at the ranch house in the years to come.

Judge Benjamin Hayes, along with his son Chauncey, were frequent visitors to Rancho Guajome. He often talked about how lively the Couts's children were. On one evening he described the following:

> Poor Cuevas, the youngest son, whom Couts loves best, was "in Coventry" at our arrival. The father had just sent him to sit in the corner for quarreling with little Nancy. Father and son both forgot the matter when Chauncey delivered him the marbles of a dozen colors brought from Los Angeles. Soon Billy and sweet María Antonia joined Cuevas and Chauncey, and I left them to their amusement under the porch.

Cave Johnson Couts served his community in many ways. He was a member of San Diego's premiere grand jury, was a county judge presiding over the probate court, and was designated to the office of the Justice of the Peace. The late Couts was also known to have a belligerent temper. He went to court for abusing a Native American, and in Old Town in 1865, also shot and killed Juan Mendoza, Rancho

Guajome's majordomo and a Mexican Revolutionary. Apparently Juan threatened Cave Couts on many occasions; however, there has not been much evidence to verify this.

You will read in the section on Rancho Buena Vista Adobe that there have been intuitive based impressions there of a man by the possible name Juan Gonzalez. Is it possible that the Juan we have communicated with at the RBVA is actually the ethereal energy of Juan Mendoza? The San Diego Paranormal Research Society will conduct further research into this plausibility. Also intriguing are the intuitive impressions by the SDPRS team indicating that the Juan it has communicated with at the RBVA has a relatively gentle energy—certainly not the energy of a violent person.

Newlywed Couts soon constructed one of the most luxurious haciendas in the area, utilizing resources from the nearby deserted Mission San Luis Rey. Couts employed Luiseño Indians to help build Guajome. The 7,000-square-foot Rancho Guajome had Spanish tile, adobe, and American framework, complete with twenty-eight rooms and an enclosed 80 ft. × 90 ft. patio with a centralized fountain. If that is not enough, the entire structure also included warehouses, servants' quarters, stables, and a chapel. Couts's other additions included a bathing pool and new kitchen, both built in 1867. To cater to servants and *vaqueros*, a separate dirt courtyard, blacksmith shop, and tack room were made available. The Couts family, including their eight children, an occasional schoolmaster, a priest, and household servants, lived the premium lifestyle at Guajome, which was known as having supreme Hispanic American structural design. The family also owned Rancho Buena Vista Adobe and San Marcos Ranchos.

Interestingly, author Helen Hunt Jackson sojourned at Guajome and intertwined some of her experiences there in her book *Ramona*. In fact, Guajome's washing place was a picturesque setting in her book as the meeting place of characters Ramona and Alessandro. She wrote the romantic novel to relay how Southern California's Native Americans often dealt with poor living conditions.

On June 10, 1874, Cave Johnson Couts passed away, ultimately leaving Rancho Guajome to Ysidora. She had much difficulty keeping it running for many years thereafter. After her death, Cave Couts Jr. inherited the property. In 1856, the young Couts was born at Guajome. Called the "last of the Dons" in San Diego County, he kept up with Spanish hospitality as much as he could. In 1924, he made some changes to the property, as its structure was weakening. His renovations consisted of guest apartments, bathrooms, sheds, garages, and new electric wiring and plumbing. He is credited with laying out the streets of Oceanside, California, during his short stint as a surveyor. At eighty-seven years old, Couts Jr. eventually passed away on July 15, 1943. The next proprietor was rancho maid Mrs. Ida Richardson, friend of the younger Couts.

Rancho Guajome later landed in the hands of San Diego County in 1973. Renovations were done, restoring it to the 1890s. As a designated National Historic Landmark (April 15, 1970) it brilliantly depicts early California American history, as well as Native American and Mexican/Californio times. In November 1936, the ranch homestead was listed as California State Landmark No. 940.

The historical significance of Rancho Guajome is equally as rich as Rancho Buena Vista Adobe. Thus, it is no surprise to find out that Guajome also has documented cases of paranormal activity. Unlike Rancho Buena Vista Adobe, paranormal researchers are not currently allowed to conduct investigations inside its premises, but that does not diminish the claims of ghostly events at the rancho house.

It would not be too far off to assume that similar types of paranormal activity occur at Guajome, especially considering it has a similar history to Rancho Buena Vista Adobe and housed some of the same families. With this said, there is probably a lot of residual energy left over at Guajome that comes in the form of disembodied voices and conversations, fleeting apparitions, footsteps, and typical day-in-the-life-of-a-rancho smells.

Circulating in the ethers are the possible apparitional sightings of Ysidora Bandini de Couts. Her husband constructed the chapel for her around 1868, so the family could have religious services there. The late Ysidora was a devout individual, and was accustomed to attending spiritual ceremonies in her childhood years. Knowing this about her makes the alleged theory that she haunts her chapel in modern times all that more sincere and veritable.

As with other noted locations in San Diego, think about the Native Americans' time on the land, as well as the Luiseños' time at Guajome; they leave another indelible mark on the city's history. Thus, they provide an additional layer of residual spiritual energy to the land, contributing to the overall picture of ethereal activity at both ranchos.

Chapter 23: Rancho Buena Vista Adobe

The San Diego Paranormal Research Society gives its monthly "Spirits of the Adobe" tours at legendary Rancho Buena Vista Adobe.

Sadly, many Southern California land ranchos have been forgotten and have fallen into ruin over the past 150 years. In many ways, they open more doors for us to learn about the people who walked the land before us. Vista, California, is home to one of the last remaining land ranchos, one that has survived the hands of time. Known as "Beautiful View" in Spanish, Rancho Buena Vista Adobe (RBVA) is in a serene setting about thirty miles north of San Diego, where its past residents are still sharing their stories.

Over the years, the legendary property would continue to be developed into what it is today. When you arrive at the black iron entrance gates on Alta Vista Drive and proceed down the historically lined brick walkway, you end at the ivy-laced courtyard door to the adobe. Once you are there, you immediately sense the echoed vibrations from long ago. Indeed, Rancho Buena Vista Adobe is a bygone era gem situated in the very heart of Vista.

Southern California has a rich history, no doubt about it. Two hundred years ago, Native Americans roamed the land in search of food, water, and other life-sustaining ingredients. The site of an ancient Native American village, Vista's native peoples originated from the Luiseños and Diegueños tribes. Gaspar de Portolá and a group of Spaniards landed in the area in 1769, with missionaries and Native Americans joining Mission San Luis Rey. In 1845, Felipe Subria lobbied Mexican administrator Governor Pio Pico for the land. Nestled between Rancho Guajome and Rancho Vallecitos de San Marcos, the 1,184.9 acres of land later became known as Rancho Buena Vista.

The Californio rancho buildings were constructed using adobe bricks, helping them last for many years. The RBVA was once part of the sprawling Mission San Luis Rey grazing lands. The structure's oldest buildings date to 1850. The original 1,184.9-acre land grant was distributed in 1845, by Governor Pio Pico to Felipe Subria, a Luiseño Indian. During this time Native Americans were established citizens according to Mexican law. Smaller land grants were issued to Christianized native peoples.

Felipe's daughter, Maria La Gracia, married an American soldier named William Dunn in summer 1851. After he was finished with his service duties, he decided to sojourn in the area and raise cattle. In April 1852, Dunn deeded the adobe property to Jesus Machedo for a mere $3,000. The construction of many rooms began, which officially became known as Rancho Buena Vista Adobe. In the coming years Lorenzo Soto moved on to the property and added more rooms.

Cave Johnson Couts had arrived on the land during the Mexican-American war. In 1851, he married his sweetheart, Ysidora Bandini, and later purchased Rancho Buena Vista Adobe. For many years the Couts family occupied both nearby Rancho Guajome and Rancho Buena Vista. Cave J. Couts and his wife actually sojourned at the nearby Guajome, whereas some of their children resided at Rancho Buena Vista.

Both locations served as the social hot spots of the area, with lots of food and many fiestas. Couts was a sub-Indian agent for the region, and with the aid of Native American labor constructed one of the best haciendas in the area. With the intention of raising cattle and livestock, Mr. Couts's herd jumped to the thousands. His son, Cave Couts Jr., would often stay overnight on the property to prevent bandits from stealing the horses.

Chalmers Scott, the family's attorney, married Maria Antonia Couts, the late Couts's eldest daughter. Cave Couts Sr. and his wife, Ysidora Bandini de Couts, later transferred the entire property to Scott and Maria in 1876. They also remodeled the adobe by adding on to two of the original structures. They can also be credited with the added vineyard and citrus orchards. The Scotts lived at Guajome the majority of the time, but also sojourned in Rancho Buena Vista Adobe. In fact, one of their eleven children was born at the latter-mentioned rancho. Deeding the RBVA to Ysidora Fuller Couts, the Scotts later moved a few miles south to San Diego.

Ysidora Fuller Couts Gray was Maria Antonia's sister who married Judge George Fuller in 1905. Mr. Fuller passed away at the RBVA in 1916. After her husband's passing young Ysidora relocated north to Los Angeles. She later died in 1952.

One of Vista's last remaining land ranchos, Rancho Buena Vista Adobe is a popular location for weddings and educational events.

In the late 1880s, other ranchos, avocado, and citrus groves became prolific, which had a direct affect on new booming small businesses in the area. The adobe itself also had some new changes. Ysidora Fuller Couts Gray and her husband previously added on the kitchen and dining room. After her husband's passing in 1918, Ysidora sold the sprawling property to F. Jack Knight and his wife, Helen Louise, one of the heirs of the well-known Mary McKinley Gold Mine in Cripple Creek, Colorado. Since the location had decreased to a mere fifty-one acres, Mr. Knight spent a good chunk of money to make improvements and renovations to the adobe, which still exists today. With the Knight's land donation adjacent Wildwood Park was developed, and is also still in use today.

Once remarried, Knight sold the adobe in 1931, to silent film producer and Metro-Golden-May Company executive Harry Pollard and silent screen legend Margarita Fischer Pollard. Making more than ninety movies, Margarita commenced her acting career at the tender age of eight. The Pollards spent $150,000 to renovate Rancho Buena Vista Adobe. They brought in various art pieces from Mexico and Europe, and the tiles for the floors and bathrooms were brought in from Italy. The dilapidated walls were reinforced and new roof tiles were installed. The patio area was even transformed into a colorful flower garden, and additions to Chalmer Scott's citrus orchards were completed. The Pollards lavishly entertained those from the Hollywood industry. One can see why the Rancho Buena Vista is considered one of the best renovated and restored land ranchos to date.

Additionally, to cater to their love of friendly gatherings, the Pollards also added on a guest house, complete with three bedrooms and 2.5 bathrooms. Today, the area serves as a gallery and office where various art pieces are displayed. The SDPRS team also commences its "Spirits of the Adobe" tours in this facility, where guests also enjoy watching a ten-minute historical video about the rancho and its past owners.

Active in the Vista community, Margarita lived in a similar style hacienda and was the founding woman of the Vista Rancheros Historical Society. After her husband's death in 1934, Margarita continued to live on the property for several more years. Mr. Frederick H. Reid of Las Vegas, Nevada, became the subsequent owner after Margarita sold it to him for $85,000. He also made renovations to the property totaling $25,000.

The adobe saw several more owners prior to the final proposal to sell it to the City of Vista. With escrow approved on July 10, 1989, the City of Vista held the adobe in its hands. Today weddings, tours, and educational programs take place at Rancho Buena Vista Adobe. The Friends of the Rancho Buena Vista oversees the gift shop and historical tours. In 2012, SDPRS worked with the City of Vista to establish a set of historical and paranormal fundraising tours at the adobe. These two-hour monthly expeditions start at 7:00 p.m. and 9:30 p.m. The SDPRS team has received critical acclaim for these tours and often sees repeat guests from all over the county.

Paranormal Experiences at RBVA

The SDPRS team has conducted a wide variety of paranormal research cases over the past years, including private residences, businesses, and historical investigations. We know that history and the paranormal share a kinship; you really cannot have one without the other. It is for this reason, as well as others, that Rancho Buena Vista Adobe is known as one of San Diego's most haunted abodes. To date, the SDPRS team has conducted seven private research projects, in addition to hosting its popular "Spirits of the Adobe" tours for five years. The team has had personal experiences with spiritual energy, as well as captured evidence in the form of audio, photo, and video from the location.

The San Diego Paranormal Research Society (SDPRS) has been honored to host haunted history tours at the adobe for five years. These fundraising tours for the

The San Diego Paranormal Research Society has conducted paranormal investigations at the adobe for several years.

Friends of the Adobe share proper ways to conduct paranormal research, as well as offer guests the chance to participate in a live electronic voice phenomena (EVP) session, Instrumental Trans Communication (ITC) session, and a dowsing rod experiment.

Over the years, people have had various experiences while visiting the adobe's grounds. Disembodied voices and footsteps, cold spots, and apparitional sightings have all been documented. One sighting in particular occurs outside along the building's veranda, where a woman dressed in white is seen roaming the premises. She is believed to be the spiritual energy of Ysidora Bandini de Couts or Ysidora Fuller Couts Gray. My mother, Norma Strickland, described seeing the specter while looking out one of the windows in the adobe's sala. To date, many people have seen this female energy. Other visual anomalies include wispy shadow figures, a woman wearing a Victorian-era dress, a man dressed in vintage cowboy attire, and a little girl.

Another fascinating sighting occurred during one of SDPRS's private investigations in September 2015. Ali Schreiber and I were doing research in the added-on kitchen. At one point, I thought I saw a shadow figure in the dining room which could be seen from where I was standing. I noted that I saw the figure walk in a right to left fashion and proceed out the door. Ali then walked outside just to make sure it was not the security guard walking around. No one else besides the two of us was in the vicinity.

Furthermore, and more along the lines of residual energy, are the claims of phantom smells and sounds having to do with the olden days at the rancho. Some of the SDPRS team's tour guests have reported smelling horses, horse manure, and hay. Many guests have reported smelling hay in the area where the horses walked

The adobe's beautiful dining room decorated for the holiday season.

through. Additionally, others have documented hearing horses gallop and talk. Cave Couts Jr. used to keep one of his prized stallions in the original adobe room and would often complain of the smells.

On an earlier 2011 research project at the adobe, I and another investigator experienced some high strangeness in the guest house quarters. While conducting a short EVP session in the kitchen, we heard what sounded like the front door opening by itself. Upon review of our audio, we captured an EVP of someone saying "Guests" at the exact same time we heard the door opening up of its own volition.

Later on during the investigation, we decided to conduct a vigil and EVP session in the family room. I was seated on the steps in between this area and the original adobe room. At one point I heard a little boy's voice, which was also captured on both recording devices. Could this tiny, ethereal visitor be one of the Couts's children? During this session we were both able to document disembodied conversations and footsteps.

The SDPRS team has also investigated the guest houses in the back of the main adobe. On a 2013 investigation, a few of us situated ourselves around a table in the center of the room. While conducting a collective audio session, one of the researchers facing me noticed a dark humanoid shadow figure looming behind me. Little did he know that I was feeling an extreme cold spot at the exact same time. Paranormal investigators always look for two or more pieces of corroboration, as this indicates a higher plausibility of paranormal activity.

On October 2015, while hosting the tours, I asked, "How many horses do you have?" A clear response of "three" can be heard coming through the spirit box. SDPRS's Ali Schreiber used to own Appaloosa horses, so she then followed up with, "Did you have any Appaloosa horses?" A clear response of "two" came through.

These are two examples of responses with apparent and contextual meaning.

The SDPRS team believes that both residual and intelligent energy exist at the adobe. There are several different layers of residual energy, obviously spanning the years of its existence. The team has also been fortunate to develop a rapport with some of its intelligent resident energies. Specifically, regarding both personal experience and captured evidence, we have communicated with Cave Couts Sr. and some members of his family—including sons William, Cave Couts Jr., and Robert Lee. Additionally, we have collected data of Ysidora Bandini de Couts and her daughter, Maria Antonia, along with Louis Machado Sr. and Herman Diaz, who both worked for Cave Couts during his reign at the adobe. Furthermore, we feel that both the Pollards are there from time to time, as well as late docents Claire and Clarence.

In fact, we have documented two intriguing audio captures correlating to the Pollards and Claire and Clarence, who spent time at the adobe as popular docents. On a private investigation in 2011, I was asking questions of the Pollards. At one point I said, "Thank you so much. What an honor to be able to talk to a great actress." The Ovilus X device then emitted the word "Hello." ITC (Instrumental Trans Communication) can be quite subjective; however, there is possible contextual meaning to the "Hello." The son of the City of Vista's former director of recreation and community services attended one of the "Spirits of the Adobe" tours in 2014. He also knew Claire and Clarence when they were alive. As we all gathered in the sala for a collective EVP session, he asked if Claire and Clarence were present with us. About two seconds later, the Ovilus X device delivered a response of "Claire." Keep in mind that the Ovilus does not keep a dictionary of people's names. Therefore, whenever a name comes through on its "Dictionary Mode" it is quite interesting, especially if there is a strong connection, as was the case in this scenario.

More Instrumental Trans Communication (ITC) Results at RBVA

In the past two years, we have seen an increased amount of spirit communication while conducting ITC experiments on our tours. ITC work can be quite subjective; thus, we look for context and direct answers to our questions. In fact, we have heard the names "Luis" and "Juan" come through the Sangean ITC device after we ask who is with us at the time. Luis Machado Sr. worked for Cave Couts, so there may be a connection there.

There is a spiritual presence at the adobe named Juan Gonzalez, whose remains are said to have been found in the majordomo room by an electrician who was in the process of installing electric wiring in the 1930s. No one knows to date who Juan is; however, he is said to have a connection to the adobe, either as a former worker or Native American servant. Here are a few examples having to do with Juan Gonzalez, which are also available on our website at http://www.sandiegoparanormalresearch.com/rancho-buena-vista-adobe-tours.html:

The San Diego Paranormal Research Society has communicated with several of the adobe's resident spirits.

1. December 2015 tour: Nicole asks, "Juan, are you in here?" A response of "Sí" clearly comes through the ITC device.

2. December 2014 tour: SDPRS's Ali Schreiber says, "You can use this device to tell us your name." A clear response of "Juan" comes through the spirit box.

3. May 2015: (Regarding Juan Gonzalez's possible remains in the wall inside the majordomo room) Nicole says, "Juan, I know this is a sensitive question, and I am trying not to be disrespectful. I hope I am not coming across that way. But, we really need to know, are your remains in this wall? Can you either answer "yes" or "no" please?" We then receive a clear response of "Can you see?"

4. June 2015: Prior to the tour, as I drove up to the adobe, I was getting an intuitive impression that Juan was friends with the Native Americans. It was quite a strong feeling, so I later asked about it on the 9:00 p.m. tour while in the majordomo room. My exact question was, "Juan, I have another question for you; were you friends with the Indians?" A male response comes through saying, "Still am."

5. June 2016: One of our research colleagues attended one of our tours as a guest. We were all standing in the majordomo room when he felt someone tug on his hair. He then asked, "Señor Gonzalez, are you the one who touched my hair?" A few moments afterward a clear response of "Juan" came through the ITC device.

Other past adobe residents have made themselves known via real-time communication. On various nights, the San Diego Paranormal Research Society has been able to capture a strong set of ITC clearly correlating to the adobe and its past residents. During summer 2015, while hosting our tours, I asked the question, "Ysidora, are you with us right now?" Immediately after my question a female response of "Sí" clearly came through the device. What is even more intriguing was the fact that I intuitively sensed her at the time of asking the question.

The above five clips, as well as the others mentioned in this section, are available for review on the San Diego Paranormal Research Society's main website:
Audio Page: http://sandiegoparanormalresearch.com/audio.html
Video Page: http://sandiegoparanormalresearch.com/video.html

On another tour, one of our team members asked if there were any adobe residents present, and shortly after the question a female response came through, answering "Maria," indicating a possible connection to Maria Antonia Couts. During one of our October 2015 tours we asked, "Is there someone with us?" Immediately the name "Herman" came through on Ali's Sangean ITC device. I then followed with, "Can you tell us your last name, please?" The name "Diaz" then came through the spirit box. Furthermore, I looked at one of the historical photos on the wall in the majordomo room, displaying a picture showing several men standing next to each other. The photo shows both Luis Machado Sr. and a man by the name Herman Diaz! Speaking of Luis, he has come through various times for us, and we are even starting to recognize the pattern of his voice. The same goes for Juan Gonzalez and Ysidora Bandini de Couts.

We have a theory as to why we are continuously capturing consistent evidence at the adobe. You see, the SDPRS team has spent some considerable amount of time on its historic premises, conducting private investigations as well as hosting monthly tours. We feel that the resident energies have come to know and trust us. Additionally, we are highly respectful and reverent to the property and its spiritual inhabitants. Perhaps they know this and can recognize that we come to their home with good intentions. As they say, the more positive and respectful energy you put out, the more you will get back.

We are continuing our "Spirits of the Adobe" tours in the years to come. It is a very fulfilling notion to know that the money generated from these fundraising events goes to Friends of the Adobe. Additionally, the tours help the rancho to keep turning the pages of its celebrated past. In a way, our tours and time spent there add more pages to its colorful history. If you visit San Diego and want to learn about the history of Vista and its ranchos, then I highly recommend stopping by Rancho Buena Vista Adobe, where the vibrations of the past can be felt in the present.

For more information, please visit, http://www.ci.vista.ca.us/residents/rancho-buena-vista-adobe. The adobe also offers fascinating daytime historical tours, as well as educational programs for school-aged children. The grounds are also a prime location to get married!

Chapter 24: San Pasqual Battlefield

Historical San Pasqual Battlefield is nestled in the hills close to the iconic San Diego Zoo Safari Park, formerly known as the Wild Animal Park. Its museum is across the street from the battle grounds. When you drive up to the location, you can feel its history vibrating all around you.

The native people lived in San Pasqual for thousands of years before they were mandated to get off of their land after the passing of their leader, Pedro Jose Panto. In the 1700s, the majority of them congregated into the San Luis Rey and San Diego missions. In 1834, after mission secularization came into effect, the San Pasqual Indian pueblo began, with natives inhabiting the San Pasqual valley. The Native Americans showcased a variety of skills and talents, working as blacksmiths, millers, leather workers, cheese makers, etc.

In 1817, Pedro Jose Panto Escarcar was baptized at the ripe age of fourteen at the San Diego Mission. He played a pivotal role in helping his native comrades after the Mexican-American War of 1846–1848. January 7, 1852, was a special day, as it marked the beginning of a "treaty of peace and friendship" between the United States and San Diego-based Diegueño (Kumeyaay) Indians. It was Panto who signed this treaty, helping to protect the tribes from exploitation from the newcomers. After his sudden death in 1874, more squatters infiltrated the area, ultimately displacing the Native Americans.

In 1883, Father Antonio Ubach, Catholic priest in San Diego, described the San Pasqual lands and how its natives were coerced off their land in 1878:

> San Pascual 17 years ago (1866) had a population of 300 souls with more than 600 acres of very good agricultural lands; it is not occupied by more than 20 squatters that with the rifle in hand scare away the Indians, not leaving one. Whisky and brutal force; nothing but the cemetery and chapel left. The few Indians that were left, two years ago had to go away and live among rocky mountains like wild beasts; there are no lands in this vicinity for the Indian.

Three military forces came together near San Pasqual. One unit contained Andres Pico and his eighty to one hundred native Californios. It was their mission to overthrow the American side, led by Archibald Gillepsie, a much smaller group hailing from San Diego. A courier from Warner's Ranch shared that the third unit included 110 United States dragoons led by Gen. Stephen Watts Kearny.

The day before the deadly battle, Kearny's men met up with Gillepsie's men. Both groups were physically exhausted from their journey through cold rain, but it did not prevent Kearny from going through with his immediate decision to attack the

Californios. After another arduous ten-mile trek, the American men located the opponents' camp fires.

The Battle of San Pasqual commenced in the foggy, early morning hours of December 6, 1846. It is noted in California history as being the most brutal and bloodiest crusade. At the time Pio Pico was the last Mexican governor of California. He led his Californios to combat against Gen. Stephen Kearny's United States Army. The entire confrontation lasted about ten minutes. Amid all of the expletives, screams, and animal noises, an American naval officer fired a howitzer (type of gun) and scared the Californios, causing them to run away from the battlefield.

At the onset of the battle, the fearful Native Americans rapidly pushed toward the mountains and watched the infamous war from a distance. At one point, Panto sent a message to Pio Pico, telling him to leave the American men alone, or else the Native Americans would intervene on their behalf.

Felicita, daughter of Capitan Pedro Jose Panto, relayed the following regarding the notorious crusade:

> The Americans did not shoot their guns many times: perhaps the rain had made the powder wet. They struck with their guns and used the sword, while the Mexicans used their long lances and their riatas [lassoing ropes]. The mules that the Americans rode were frightened and ran all through the willows by the river. After them rode the Mexicans on their swift horses, striking with the lance and lassoing with the riata; it was a very terrible time.

As a result of the war, California became part of the United States and no longer belonged to Mexico. This resulted in the arrival of many people wishing to settle in this new territory. In the aftermath of the tragic scene, eighteen Americans lay silently on the ground, devoid of any life. In fact, the majority of American officers were either injured or dead. Gen. Kearny sustained two lance wounds. Once the sun set and the stars shined, the official count of the deceased increased to nineteen American souls as another soldier succumbed to his wounds. They were all buried underneath a willow tree.

In reality, there was no rhyme or reason why San Pasqual was chosen as the ultimate battlefield. The Americans, along with Kearny, displayed an unrealistic sense of tragic optimism, a sentiment that precipitated the Mexican-American War. Perhaps if the men had acted more strategically less pain would have ensued and more lives would have been saved.

Battlefields are some of the most haunted places on Earth. Think about all of the pain, suffering, and death ultimately leaving imprinted emotions on the environment. When you read about this bloodiest battle in California's history, it is not at all surprising that spiritual energy exists on its front lines. Most often residual paranormal energy or psychic imprints of days past occur at these locations.

In the case of San Pasqual Battlefield, there have been several reports of apparitions adorned in clothing reminiscent of both the Californio and American sides. Some people have documented seeing the specters of men fighting each other on the exact spot where the bloody mess took place. Again, this is most likely an imprint of the tragedy replaying itself over and over. People have also reported hearing the disembodied screams and cries of men, but there is no one around to justify the sounds. Yet again, this is another sign of the residual sounds of suffering from years past.

The San Diego Paranormal Research Society took a field trip to the San Pasqual grounds about five years ago. We hiked up a small pathway across the way from the actual battlefield and took a few moments of silence to remember the fallen souls from that fateful December day many years ago. After a while we decided to conduct a short EVP session. There was little wind, and the animals at the adjacent Safari Park were very quiet, so the outside environment was quite suitable for an audio session.

We asked questions in English and Spanish. At one point I asked, "Whose men are here, Pio Pico's or Kearny's?" None of us heard any audible response from that question; however, upon review of my audio a few days later, I heard something that sent chills up and down my body. You see, about two seconds after I asked the above question I captured a man's voice loudly answering, "Pico."

We encountered a couple freezing cold spots on our excursion as well. Seeing as it was a warm day, it seemed quite unusual. Was there a ghostly energy there, drawing heat from the environment to manifest? Quite possibly, yes. A couple team members also noted hearing footsteps from time to time. We thoroughly looked around us, and we were the only people on the trail at the time. Was it possible that we heard an animal? Maybe, but the noises we heard sounded as though they came from someone wearing shoes.

The battlefield's museum has an abundance of historical resources pertaining to the San Pasqual lands and its noted battle. When you visit its premises plan to stay for a few hours. There are even some picnic benches outside where you can take a break and have some lunch in the welcoming California weather. Before you leave, take some time and commemorate the lost souls who fought for their freedom many years ago.

PART VIII:
West County San Diego's Most Haunted

There are various historic sites situated among San Diego's picturesque coastline that have a reputation for housing a spirit or two. For one, the western portion of San Diego County is home to the Hotel Del Coronado, one of the most talked about ornate hotels in the world. In fact, one cannot visit San Diego without traveling over the iconic Coronado Bridge and spending the day at the Victorian American Queen Anne-inspired structure. From hotels to racetracks to restaurants, the city's western region continues to share its historical past with visitors from all over the globe.

Chapter 25: Del Mar Fairgrounds and Racetrack

The Del Mar area is considered one of the most beautiful and picturesque locations in the entire Pacific coastal region. The origins of Del Mar began with a man by the name of Theodore M. Loop and his wife Ella. In 1882, he obtained some land and constructed a residence on the north shore of Los Peñasquitos Creek. He built a tent city on Torrey Pines State Beach, with Ella eventually naming it "Del Mar." In fact, these two words originated from a well-known poem, *The Fight on Paseo Del Mar*.

Later that year, Col. Jacob Taylor traveled to the area with his family with the hopes of settling on Rancho Peñasquitos. Eventually, Loop and Taylor jointly decided to construct a town, mainly due to its aesthetic charm and commercial potential. During the summer months of 1885, Taylor procured 338.11 acres from Enoch Talbert for $1,000 along the mesa's north end, signaling the birth of Del Mar.

Taylor depicted Del Mar as being a model seaside resort for renowned wealthy people. With the technical assistance of friends and family, he devised and constructed a town whose main attraction was Casa del Mar, a hotel and vacation destination. Other tourist spots included a train station, dance hall, and bathing pool. Sadly, Casa del Mar burned to the ground in 1889, and several locals dealt with economic adversities which had a direct affect on the area. For the ensuing fifteen years, the town became quiescent until the early 1900s, when the South Coast Land Company's expansion of San Diego County began.

Del Mar was officially incorporated into a city by 1959. The establishment of the University of California San Diego (UCSD) directly influenced the coastal town's cultural, political, and social life. From the latter 1960s to the early 1980s, residents were dedicated to improving the city's environment. Due to its innately attractive ambience Del Mar became home to those with creative thumbs. Known as the "Crown Jewel of San Diego," Del Mar offers various boutique shops, delectable restaurants, and prized tourist attractions.

In 1933, people sought out a permanent site for the San Diego County Fair. San Diego community leaders James E. Franks and Frank G. Forward visited Sacramento to persuade Gov. James Rolph Jr. to approve the building of an everlasting fair location. It was Ed Fletcher who felt that the 184 acres of land in the San Dieguito Valley would be best suited for a fairground. The Works Progress Administration (WPA) supplied the initial capital, and on October 8, 1936, the Del Mar Fair opened its doors to an energized crowd of 50,000 people.

Prior to building the Del Mar Racetrack, those residing in Southern California flocked to the Agua Caliente Racetrack in Tijuana, Mexico. People reveled in drinking and gambling at the track down south that attracted celebrities and affluent individuals. Eventually gambling was forbidden in Mexico; however, during the mid-1930s, many areas in the United States opened their doors again to the sport. In fact, the Great Depression's impact on California's economy led to a movement that legalized horse racing. The race track's opening day on July 3, 1937, signaled a new period for Del Mar. The ensuing years brought thousands of people to Del Mar. From residents to well-known celebrities, such as Desi and Lucy Arnaz, people flocked to the picturesque town.

With the establishment of the mile-long racetrack, Bing Crosby created the Del Mar Turf Club with Pat O'Brien serving as vice president. Having owned several race horses in Rancho Santa Fe, Mr. Crosby fronted $250,000 for the construction of the track and the grandstands. On the racetrack's debut day, he broadcast a forty-minute NBC radio show that included his dedicated song "Where the Surf Meets the Turf" and celebrity interviews.

According to *Images of America: Del Mar Fairgrounds*, the San Diego County Fair officially opened on October 8, 1936. The 50,000 attendees enjoyed a variety of entertainment, rides, exhibits, and fun contests. Inside the tents were stunt artists, sideshows, and food vendors. Several types of attractions lit up the area, including daredevil motorcycle riders, circus and vaudeville acts, children's programs, and the famous "Slide for Life," where a human flew through space while on a wire. Organized primarily as a summer event, the following 1937 fair ran from August 7 through August 15.

With the outbreak of World War II the racetrack closed its doors, with its grandstands serving as a bomber tail assembly production facility. Temporary military personnel quarters were on the grounds, with other areas laid out for Camp Elliot US Marine training. On July 1, 1943, eighty acres east of the fairgrounds were reserved as an airship landing location. With the departure of the Marines and paratroopers, 500,000 square feet of empty space was utilized for the development of B-17 "Flying Fortress" bomber parts. The United States entered the war when the Japanese attacked Pearl Harbor, temporarily halting fairs and racing.*

The San Diego County Fair recommenced in 1946. For the ensuing four decades, Don Diego served as the county fair's most familiar symbol, as he was known for his grand parties. His image was used in advertisements and promotions. In fact, the character depiction was based on the real-life Don Diego Alvarado, whose family had a substantial Del Mar land grant in the latter portion of the 1800s. For four decades Tommy Hernandez played the role of the fair's iconic mascot. In addition to Don Diego, the fair's promotion department created the Fairest of the Fair Pageant.

* Sadly, Army pilot Lt. Col. John Coleman Herbst passed away when his P-80 jet fighter crashed during an air show maneuver on July 4, 1946.

Known as one of the world's top ten events, the San Diego County Fair sees an average of 1.3 million visitors during its annual July run.

Working in unison, the Del Mar Fairgrounds and the Del Mar Fair commenced the substantial mission to redesign the original grandstand in 1991. Those directly involved in this undertaking worked hard to highlight the structure's Spanish Revival theme. Fourteen artists were chosen to supply and decorate the interior areas with a primordial Spanish-Indian appearance. Many of the selected fountains and furniture items hailed from Mexico, showcasing a graceful Spanish design.

Today, the Del Mar Fairgrounds offers more than just fast horses, flower shows, livestock contests, sporting events, celebrity appearances, carnival rides, and delectable food; the historic location is also reputed to have a haunted history. Paranormal researchers agree that supernatural activity is attracted to places that have seen a substantial stream of human traffic over the years. Those visiting the fairgrounds exude excitement, and even anxiety when placing a bet on a horse. Could all of this impacted human emotion from many years somehow naturally charge spiritual energy? It is also theorized that renovation can cause or increase ghostly activity, and we know that the structure went through a massive overhaul. Is it possible that spirit energy is attached to some of the furniture pieces imported from Mexico? There can even be some residual imprints left over from the World War II days, and even during the Native American period as well.

There have been many claims of ghostly energy swirling throughout the grandstands. A local San Diego-based paranormal research team has conducted several projects in various areas of the fairgrounds. One of the common claims from employees is hearing disembodied vocalizations in the grandstands. Whether this is a residual phenomenon, or perhaps human conversations bleeding in from other areas, remains to be seen. Even the sounds of phantom hooves have been heard on the track. Shadow figures have been seen fleeting around, as well as ghostly specters clad in vintage attire. There have also been reports of sightings of deceased celebrities in the grandstands.

The grandstands' fifth floor and second-level bar seem to be hot spots for paranormal activity. A night club populated by celebrities in the 1930s formerly existed on the fifth floor. Staff members have found furniture items moved to different locations. Even doors have been reported to open and shut of their own volition. Striking cold spots have been felt in various hallway areas. The sounds of disembodied glasses clinking together has been heard, in addition to phantom smells of cigar smoke. I talked with one researcher who has investigated the grandstand area. A ghostly male vocalization was uttered as the group was conducting a mock poker game with the intent of triggering ghostly happenings. This person relayed that this invisible male specter commented on the group's simulated game.

Since I am a native San Diegan, I have visited the Del Mar Fairgrounds on numerous occasions. The entire edifice and its surroundings emanate complete nostalgia. In my opinion, it seems as though its paranormal activity is a mixture of intelligent and residual energy. On many occasions I have felt extreme cold spots and a general thickness in certain hallways. I have talked to some people who have had odd occurrences in the bathrooms, such as hearing someone in the adjacent stalls when no one else is there.

Since I have never officially conducted a ghost research project at the Del Mar Fairgrounds, I cannot honestly say whether or not it is actually haunted. However, the sources that I have consulted for the purposes of this book strongly feel that it is a paranormal hot spot. Many of the aforementioned theories can potentially explain the genesis of the location's supernatural energy. Then again, there may be those elusive reasons that we mortals do not yet know, or are not permitted to know until we pass on.

Chapter 26: Hotel Del Coronado

Hotel Del Coronado is one of San Diego's most popular tourist destinations.

In 1846, Don Pedro Carrillo obtained 4,100 acres via a Spanish land grant. At the time, the Coronado peninsula was a barren land with shrubs and weeds. After California became part of the United States, Don Pedro sold the terrain in 1849, for a mere $1,000. After the termination of the Civil War, the land was purchased for $10,000.

As Coronado's most prized edifice, the Hotel Del Coronado is perhaps one of the most historic structures to ever be erected in the state of California. With its many years of service, it is quite surprising that the historical landmark has only seen six owners. Elisha Babcock Jr. was the premiere proprietor of the prized structure. Along with his family members, he arrived in San Diego from Evansville, Indiana, in 1884. A railroad executive, he was coerced into premature retirement due to failing health. However, his vision for developing the hotel remained strong and healthy.

Babcock and his friend, H. L. Story, soon realized the opportunities that lay ahead for this intriguing stretch of land. With the railroad readily reaching San Diego, the two men recognized that this exquisite piece of land could attract people from all walks of life to the city's admired weather and climate. Both men developed a syndicate referred to as the Coronado Beach Company, with the ultimate objective to purchase the peninsula and develop a thriving city. Furthermore, they envisioned building a luxurious hotel with the organization's profits. Once the premiere transcontinental railroad reached the Mohave Desert community of Barstow in 1885, Babcock and Story bought the Coronado peninsula for $110,000 in December of that year—a mere sum by today's standards.

Soon after, the land was being developed and arranged to accommodate their vision. A railroad line was extended, which ran along the Silver Strand peninsula. In addition to a pipeline, transportation systems, and neighborhood construction, the two men constructed one of California's initial power plants, providing power to the entire Coronado community until 1922.

Soon promotional events took place, mainly to advertise San Diego as one of the most attractive places in the nation to live and visit. Babcock relayed that he desired to develop a resort that would ultimately be known as the "talk of the Western world." On Independence Day 1886, a community picnic celebration was underway, signaling the start of a yearly tradition that still exists today. The Reid Brothers were the chosen architects for the envisioned hotel and resort. On November 13, 1886, approximately 6,000 individuals took a boat trip to the Coronado Beach Company's complementary picnic lunch.

It was originally announced that the grand hotel would be ready by the following November, but delays postponed its opening day to mid-December. As the hotel's construction came to an end, the US economy system endured difficult times.

For the next forty years, local pioneers worked collectively to establish a contemporary city. When John D. Spreckels arrived in San Diego, he became fascinated by the City of Coronado and its prized new structure. Babcock persuaded Spreckels to financially subsidize the Coronado Beach Company. As years passed, he managed the corporation and hotel via his San Francisco residence.

From June through December 1902, the Hotel Del Coronado closed its doors to receive further renovations. This, in turn, signaled the beginning of Coronado's famed Tent City along the Silver Strand, a huge social arena for Coronado's residents. There were many activities to choose from, including boating ventures, concerts, plays, and vaudeville shows. In 1939, Tent City's era of vacation paradise officially ended.

After the San Francisco earthquake, Spreckels and his family moved to San Diego and resided at the hotel until their sprawling mansion was constructed. Spreckels guided the hotel through one of its most exquisite eras. After the Great Depression he sold some properties but held on to the grand edifice. It eventually went up for sale after World War II ended. At this point "The Del," as it is affectionately known, was not the symbol of opulence it once portrayed.

As time went on the structure saw more owners, including Kansas City hotel mogul Barney Goodman, who commenced further renovations of the building. With Goodman's restoration vision a fifth floor was added, as well as another fifty rooms. Furthermore, the hotel's exterior and interior portions received upgrades. Sadly, Mr. Goodman passed away in 1951, which had a direct affect on the hotel, as refurbishments were curtailed.

Local entrepreneur John S. Alessio took over ownership of the Del in 1961. As with his predecessor, he also set his eyes on restoration projects. With this plan public areas and guest rooms were greatly improved. The original windows inside the Crown and Coronet rooms were detached and replaced with massive plate glass pieces that are still visible today.

Prior to the completion of Alessio's renovation, the Hotel Del Coronado Corporation purchased the structure from Alessio some years later. M. Larry Lawrence served as the board's chairman and became the Del's sixth proprietor. With his design proposal, it would be restored to its innate Victorian grandeur and as an eye-catching backdrop for San Diego's social arena. He built the Grande Hall, appealing to large groups due to its ability to hold 1,500 persons. Additionally, the number of guest rooms increased from 399 to 689 as a result of the Ocean Towers and pool side development. Interestingly, when the Hotel Del Coronado Corporation took over, many aspects of the hotel were in bad shape; many of its mechanical and electrical components did not function properly. Between 1963 and 1983, $40 million was allocated for restoring, repairing, and replacing defunct systems. With Lawrence's vision the structure gained more influence as a resort and convention center.

As one of the last remaining luxurious seaside resorts, the Hotel Del Coronado serves as a symbol of past times. The Hotel Del Coronado is a perfect depiction of the Victorian era. In fact, the Crown Room dining area is one of the nation's most awe-inspiring architectural milestones. Today, the grand structure is one of San Diego's most popular tourist destinations. Guests and locals alike can partake in a stroll along the beach, dine at one of the building's prized eateries, or shop in many of its boutique stores. To be honest, one cannot visit "America's Finest City" without visiting the grand Victorian structure, her red-roofed turrets visible as you drive along the streets of Coronado.

There are usually stories of ghosts and spirits associated with aged hotels, and the Hotel Del Coronado is no exception. Many people have experienced otherworldly phenomena while visiting the historic building. With occasional apparitional sightings, cold spots, and disembodied voices, the Del is known as one of San Diego's most haunted locations.

The story of Kate Morgan is perhaps the most popular spirited tale associated with the edifice. Kate Kathleen Farmer was born in Iowa on September 23, 1865, to George W. Farmer, an affluent miller and his wife, Elizabeth, who passed away shortly after giving birth. Having no surviving brothers or sisters, Kate was then primarily brought up by the males in her life, and it has been suggested that as a result, she turned out to be rambunctious and uncontrollable. In her late teens, Kate wed Tom Morgan on December 30, 1885, and the couple had one child by the name of Thomas who passed away just two days after his birth.

In 1892, on Thanksgiving Day, the young and beautiful Ms. Morgan checked into the Del under the alias "Lottie A. Bernard." She was alone and despondent when she arrived, having waited five lonesome days, possibly for her husband Tom

Morgan. Sadly, just five days later, Kate was found lifeless on one of the exterior staircases leading to the beach. She was found to have a single gunshot wound to the temple, and it was later ruled that she committed suicide. The news of her demise became a national sensation, as her description and circumstances were telegraphed to police personnel around the nation. Tom sent a letter to the San Diego coroner identifying Lottie A. Bernard as Kate Morgan. The letter mentioned that her Iowa-based grandfather was Joe W. Chandler, and that he should be the one to receive her remains.

The situation surrounding Kate Morgan's short stay at the Hotel Del Coronado continues to remain quite ambiguous to this day. Thus, the events preceding her tragic demise are not entirely based in fact, leading people to infer and formulate their own conclusions as to what transpired.

The coroner's inquest took place on November 30, just one day after her youthful body was found. Witness testimonies have provided in-depth information about her actions and behavior during her sojourn at the Hotel Del Coronado. At the time of her stay Kate seemed to be ill and depressed, and told hotel staff she was suffering from stomach cancer, possibly concealing the fact that she may have been pregnant. Oddly, she told employees to not worry about her condition, as her brother, who happened to be a doctor, was soon to arrive to help her. Kate even approached the front desk several times asking about her brother and when he was to arrive. As it turns out, this young, beautiful woman never had a brother; thus, most people feel that the man she was anxiously awaiting was in fact her husband Tom.

It was determined that Kate Morgan resided in and worked at the Los Angeles home of L. A. Grant, where she went by the alias "Katie Logan." She was reported to be a sufficient employee, always tending to her assigned duties. Her husband was known to be a gambler, a fact that concerned her at times. Another oddity is evident, in that she left for San Diego without her personal belongings, therefore suggesting she would soon return to Los Angeles.

As she traveled by train to San Diego, witness accounts disclosed that a woman matching her physical description quarreled with a man who left her en route. One of these eye-witnesses was a man named Joseph E. Jones, who documented that Kate and a man had a significant altercation. The man got off the train in Orange County, whereas Kate continued south toward San Diego.

Many rumors have circulated around Kate's tragic death and still do so to this day. Almost immediately people wondered why she traveled to the ornate hotel alone, something that women of her time period rarely did. Some say she wanted to divorce Tom, especially since witnesses declared that she wanted to get some papers signed. It has been speculated that she committed suicide; however, others feel that she was the victim of a senseless crime.

Mrs. Morgan visited a gun shop in San Diego and purchased a .44 Bulldog. She may have arrived back at the Del between 6:00 p.m. and 7:00 p.m later that night. A witness spotted her standing on her room's veranda as she gazed toward the stormy Pacific Ocean. Perhaps her husband finally arrived at the hotel, where the couple further argued; however, the condition of her hotel room did not indicate a struggle of any kind. If Tom and Kate did argue, maybe he fired his gun at her head, ultimately ending her life. This scenario seems quite plausible.

Alan M. May, author of *The Legend of Kate Morgan: The Search for the Ghost of the Hotel Del Coronado*, discusses significant clues that strongly signify that Kate was in fact murdered. You see, the medical examiner testified that the bullet found lodged in Kate's forehead came from a .38 or .40 caliber weapon, a bullet commonly associated with the Derringer gun that Tom carried on his person. Additionally, Kate was found to have been shot in the temple at an upward angle, indicating that she was standing a couple stairs above her assailant. The trajectory of her wound would have been entirely different if Kate had shot herself with her gun. Also, the positioning of her body on the staircase was not indicative of a self-inflicted wound, as she would have fallen in a downward direction. Kate was found on the stairs with her head toward the top and her feet toward the bottom of the stairs. Furthermore, her pistol was oxidized the following day, suggesting that her attacker washed his bloody hands in the saltwater ocean, then came back and strategically placed the gun underneath her hand so it looked like she committed the act.

As already mentioned, at the time of her unfortunate demise law enforcement was not able to locate anything to positively identify her, so a depiction of Kate was telegraphed to police agencies throughout the nation. Known to newspapers as the "Beautiful Stranger," Mrs. Morgan was an unhappily married woman and worked for an affluent family in Los Angeles. She was buried at Mt. Hope Cemetery in San Diego.

According to *Beautiful Stranger: The Ghost of Kate Morgan and the Hotel del Coronado*, numerous hotel guests have documented high strangeness, specifically in Mrs. Morgan's original room on the third floor. In 1892, the room she stayed in was numbered 302, whereas today it is number 3327. Some of the acknowledged experiences include flickering lights, cold spots, phantom scents, disembodied voices and footsteps, opening and closing doors, and people's belongings moving around. The bed in Kate's room often shows an imprint, as if someone was lying in it. Even the television is reported to turn on and off sometimes, but that can be indicative of a circuit issue. Her ethereal form has been spotted by many guests, especially in hallways and along the beach. In fact, some witnesses describe seeing a woman's spirit walk down the actual staircase where Kate's body was found.

One couple from California decided to vacation at the Hotel Del Coronado, not yet realizing that they were in for a spirited treat. While in bed, their covers were yanked off by a female form standing at the foot of it. Both parties witnessed their fan's tassel moving of its own volition. Other reported experiences from this husband and wife included doorknobs rattling and dimming lights in the bathroom. Apparently their housekeeper refused to enter the room, preferring to wait outside.

There have been other ghost sightings at the Hotel Del Coronado, including spirit forms adorned in vintage attire and paranormal activity in room 3519. Some have witnessed seeing phantom forms of men clad in antiquated suits. Intriguingly, the gift shop area is home to various supernatural experiences, where employees have documented purchase items flying off shelving units, only to land upright and in perfect condition, as well as other psychokinetic forms of activity. The hotel lobby area is also home to ghostly goings on. Concierge employees have reported hearing disembodied conversations and whispering. One staff member spotted a 1940s-clad male apparition who appeared out of nowhere. Furthermore, other hotel rooms are known to have unusual occurrences, including the sightings of residual apparitions. Intuitive individuals, including myself, have felt a general heaviness in certain areas of the hotel.

I have visited the Hotel Del Coronado on numerous occasions, and it is a pleasure every time I do so. With this said, I have experienced physical manifestations of vertigo, nausea, and flu-like symptoms in various spots inside the grand structure. Being a paranormal researcher, I strive to find logical explanations for alleged spirit activity. Thus, I surmise that the EMF in certain locations may be the cause of the aforementioned symptoms. Or has my body psychically sensed the forlorn and melancholic feelings that Kate endured during her short stay at the hotel? Perhaps it is a combination of both. Whatever the case, I hope that Kate Morgan has found eternal peace and rest. If she spiritually continues to visit the Hotel Del Coronado, I hope it is done out of pure desire and free will.

Chapter 27: Hunter Steakhouse

Oceanside is situated about forty miles northwest of San Diego, at the mouth of the San Luis Rey River. Founded by Andrew Jackson Myers, the city was incorporated on July 3, 1888. Its native inhabitants were the Luiseños, named after the King of France. Appropriately titled the "King of Missions," Mission San Luis Rey is one of the largest constructed California missions, attracting thousands of tourists on an annual basis.

Over the years, San Diego County has seen approximately 140 graveyards, ranging from small family plots to extensive cemeteries. Today only a fraction of them remain. Some are easily accessible, whereas others are hidden. At the intersection of Interstate 5 and Highway 78 lies Oceanside's first cemetery, formally known as Buena Vista Cemetery. It is postulated that approximately forty pioneers were buried here until about 1906. Some of the bodies were relocated to the newer Oceanview Cemetery, with the remaining ones sadly suffering years of neglect. Eventually, a developer purchased the land and petitioned the City of Oceanside to rezone it for business use. In 1970, it was discovered that seventeen of the remaining souls were disinterred and relocated to El Camino Memorial Park in Sorrento Valley.

Sarah Francie Parry was the first documented burial at the location in March 1888, but George Bronson's headstone was there prior to Parry's internment. In 1916, his remains were later interred adjacent to his wife in Oceanview Cemetery. The majority of Oceanside pioneers were laid to rest here. The cemetery was formed as early as 1885, and was recorded in 1888, by J. Chauncey Hayes.

Sadly, a fire erupted in 1952, and obliterated the majority of the wooden headstones. As the 1970s rolled around, the hillside was revamped to make way for a restaurant and gas station. A memorial plaque sits next to a sidewalk, listing the names of all interred. Ultimately, the rezoning of the property resulted in years of abuse and neglect, as many of the remains were exposed, unceremoniously removed, and forgotten. Perhaps the ill treatment of the grave sites and the souls who rest there serve as a foundation for the restaurant's hauntings.

Hunter Steakhouse in Oceanside dwells on the hill just above the Buena Vista Lagoon. As you can imagine, it is also placed on top of the very hill that houses the Buena Vista grave site. The popular restaurant is not just known for its delectable food and desserts; it is also one of Oceanside's spiritually inhabited hot spots. Many researchers believe that its ghostly happenings occur because it sits atop the neglected grave site. Of course, there can be other elusive reasons as well, only to become known when the time is right. Perhaps we will never know all of the motives behind its hauntings.

Many restaurant employees report odd occurrences while working at Hunter Steakhouse. They maintain that the spiritual energies are amiable, curious, and playful. One interesting experience correlating to the previously described spiritual temperaments occurred as a waiter was carrying a tray of loaded dishes. As the tray was tilting to one side, he felt an invisible force push up against it, subsequently preventing the dishes and glassware from falling off the trey. This employee strongly felt that the energy responsible for this was helpful in nature.

According to some staff, a female energy is known to appear on the stairway leading down to the bar area. The apparition of a man clad in period clothing has been corroborated by various employees. In this same area others have heard their names being called by an unseen female presence, thus indicating possible intelligent communication as opposed to residually imprinted psychic energy. Restaurant patrons have also witnessed a gliding apparition in the upstairs dining room area. The list goes on, as guests have heard their names being called by disembodied forces. Others have felt isolated cold spots not explained by air conditioning or open windows. Intriguingly, restaurant employees often experience similar types of phenomena which undoubtedly serve as corroborating events.

Furthermore, psychokinetic (PK) energy occurs, as both employees and staff report occurrences of moving items. A former female employee consistently complained that her hair was being pulled by unseen forces. Her experiences eventually led her to terminate her employment. One of the most well-known occurrences has to do with invisible forces moving the display of wine bottles. One employee actually saw a heavy box of wine move of its own volition. Doors have mysteriously closed and locked by themselves at times. Restaurant workers have documented hearing rhythmic thumping and knocking sounds emanating from the attic area, supposedly another hot spot area inside the restaurant. Witnesses have described seeing the brief sighting of a male apparition out of the chimney as well.

In 2010, the San Diego Paranormal Research Society was invited by restaurant management to conduct an after-hour investigation of Hunter Steakhouse. The minute I walked into the building I could sense a lot of energy, as the environment felt thick. In talking with management, we learned that many guests feel uncomfortable while inside the building, with many having to prematurely leave. In our opinion, some of these feelings can be attributed to the extreme EMF (electromagnetic field) levels in the building as detected via our environmental monitoring devices. Many individuals innately have an EMF sensitivity that can physically manifest in headaches, paranoia, flu-like symptoms, feelings of being watched, etc.

Electrical outages have been reported, as well as certain lights intermittently turning on and off. This is why it is important to attempt to naturally explain any occurrence prior to deeming it a supernatural phenomenon. In fact, the EMF readings were so high that we recommended a consultation with an electrician and scheduled an appointment for them to survey the building's electrical lines. It is possible that the high amounts of EMF that we detected could also serve as a capacitor for the restaurant's spiritual happenings.

The San Diego Paranormal Research Society encountered a frightening experience while in the process of conducting its overnight investigation of Hunter Steakhouse in 2010. This fearful event had nothing to do with supernatural forces; you see, two men armed with a gun burst into the kitchen with the intention of robbing the restaurant. Thankfully, the team followed its emergency protocols and was physically unharmed. It is for this very reason that every paranormal research team should have a set of emergency protocols for various disasters, such as fires, earthquakes, robberies, medical emergencies, etc.

At the time of the robbery, the team was about two hours into its investigation, divided into two teams of three individuals. One group was situated upstairs in the dining rooms, whereas the other group was in the downstairs bar area. I was in the bar and vividly remember the words coming through our two-way radios, "Guys, stay where you are, this place has just been robbed." After momentary anxiety and fear our instincts and emergency operating procedures took effect. Each group remained where they were and waited for instruction from the San Diego Police Department upon its arrival.

Once law enforcement personnel arrived we were instructed to remain on the premises, mainly for questioning purposes. Two squad cars arrived, along with a trained police dog. A helicopter was flying overhead, surveying the ground. Another important aspect of this event has to do with having written permission from the location you are investigating. The police asked to see our signed investigation permission form from restaurant management. We also had our business cards on hand. After about two hours we were able to leave the location with added emergency training under our belt and an experience to boot. Sadly, our investigation of the restaurant was interrupted, but all of us were very thankful that we were not harmed or robbed. The team has plans to return to Hunter Steakhouse to continue its paranormal research of the establishment.

It is my sincere hope that all of the souls laid to rest at Buena Vista Cemetery find eternal peace. For those remaining earthbound energies, I sincerely hope they can find the path that will lead them home.

Chapter 28: Twin Inns

When Franciscan Father Juan Crespí and military leader Don Gaspar de Portolá traveled through the area that was to become Carlsbad, Crespí remarked in his July 17, 1769, diary entry:

> We descended in to a valley full of alders, in which we saw a village, but without people. In passing we named this village San Simón de Lipnica [later changed to Agua Hedionda]. We continued on our way in the same northerly direction over hills and broad mesas supplied with good pasture and after more leagues travel we descended to a small, very green valley which has a narrow plain some varas wide [a vara equals a little less than a yard]. We pitched camp on the slope of the valley on the west side. The water is collected in pools, and we noticed that it flowed out of several springs forming about it marshes, or stagnant pools covered with rushes and grasses. We named this place Santa Sinforosa [Buena Vista]. We saw from camp a village of heathen on the summit of a hill who . . . deputed two of their number to visit us. As soon as they went back to their village all its inhabitants came to camp. Not fewer than 40 presented themselves . . .

Carlsbad, California, is a coastal community north of San Diego. Its history consists of a culmination of individual influences. Every single person who touched this area has contributed to its rich, storied past. Perhaps the earliest known days of Carlsbad can be traced to Spain's 1769 Sacred Expedition, which was commanded by Father Serra and Gaspar de Portolá. In fact, Russian intrigue in the Pacific Northwest region of the United States, along with English interest, directly influenced Spain to initiate this sacred expedition to claim the area. Its primary goals were to map geographic locations and unearth suitable establishment sites for towns and missions largely based on the number and position of the natives. Diaries document how they traveled over the road that would later become El Camino Real, as well as meeting several Native Americans who resided around the lagoons.

In the early days, the two Native American tribes—Luiseños and Diegueños (Kumeyaay)—were residing in the area when the Spanish peoples arrived. It was when Father Lausen launched the Mission San Luis Rey de Francia in 1798, that these particular natives really felt the entire impact of Spain's authority. The native folks from Baja missions traveled with the Franciscan fathers to establish the Alta California missions. Thus, the way of life changed dramatically for these northern indigenous residents.

The missions of the day employed the Native Americans to construct orchards, cattle ranches, water systems, and other various agricultural developments. They remained in their villages for the most part and traveled to the mission on a rotating basis. The native peoples assigned to this site were the only groups to survive this period in great numbers. Mission San Luis Rey was the biggest livestock ranch in the mission system, with 50,000-plus cattle and sheep. In addition to pioneering agricultural methods, the mission instituted the idea of private land ownership. Physically lasting approximately thirty years, it left an everlasting impression on cultural, social, and religious customs.

When Mexico gained its independence from Spain in 1821, these mission lands were divided and secularized. By 1834, Mexican Governor Alvarado started issuing the first private land grants from the mission lands. Thus, Mission San Luis Rey was partitioned into five individual land grants, including Aqua Hedionda, Buena Vista, Encinitas, Guajome, and Los Vallecitos de San Marcos. After the Mexican-American war ended in 1848, with Mexico losing approximately one-half of its entire terrain to the United States, a deluge of Americans entered California with one common interest: gold. The people who traveled to Southern California were mainly interested in ranching and farming. With the intent to permanently live in the area, they settled on these ranches with family members.

Robert Kelly, an emigrant from the Isle of Mann, was also influential in the development of Carlsbad. He was hired to manage operations at Rancho Agua Hedionda for a variety of reasons. He formerly co-owned a Jamacha ranch, as well as ran a mercantile in San Diego. The property was originally granted to Don Juan Maria Marron. Furthermore, Kelly served in the United States Army post war Survey Commission. After the 1870 death of Francis Hinton, Mr. Kelley solely inherited Rancho Agua Hedionda. He approved a coastal passageway to the Southern California Railway, which provided access between San Diego and north county areas. This new rail line directly initiated the development of previously unchartered and undeveloped coastal land.

In 1883, John Frazier and his family members were some of the first to arrive by train and settle in the area that he later renamed Frazier's Station. Mr. Frazier realized that water was scarce in this settled area just south of the Buena Vista Lagoon. To provide for him and his family he employed the Mull Brothers—expert well specialists—to dig a well. In 1885, water was unearthed at several hundred feet. Some sources say 245 feet, whereas others document 400 feet! Alas, mineral and artesian water were finally discovered, and as a result the value of land increased by fifty percent. Later analysis revealed that the well water in this Southern California area nearly matched that of the water from the famous "Well Number 9" in Karlsbad, Bohemia. To celebrate this intriguing fact the area's name was changed to Carlsbad, California.

The Smith-Emery Co. of Los Angeles laboratory analyzed the water's parts per million of the chemical content and concluded that the water consisted of various minerals. The California Southern Railway (Santa Fe) and the Carlsbad Land and

Mineral Water Company were directly responsible for the promotion of Carlsbad. Railway waiting areas across the nation advertised the new Carlsbad hotel, spa, and amazing waters.

In 1887, Gerhard Schutte, the land company's president, built a spacious nearby home. One of his partners, D. D. Wadsworth, also erected a house on the same block that identically matched that of his partner's. This extravagant Queen Anne edifice was assembled with lumber shipped from Nebraska. Noticeable for miles across the coastal region, these two mirror-image residences became Carlsbad landmarks.

Around 1900, the Carlsbad land boom finished, and within a few years the Carlsbad Land & Water Company was restructured. The Schutte family relocated to National City in 1906. The twin homes were leased for commercial reasons. They became known as the Twin Inns and served as renting rooms. The house saw a few owners until November 5, 1919, when specialty chef Eddie Kentner relocated to Carlsbad with the intent of purchasing the three-acre property, and he and his wife, Neva, took over the location.

Mr. Kentner was a specialty chef on the New York-to-Chicago 20th Century Limited. He then worked as a culinary specialist for Baron Long, the developer and proprietor of the Biltmore Hotel in Los Angeles. The Twin Inns were known for their skinless chicken dinner accompanied by hash brown potatoes, country gravy, fresh peas, biscuits, corn fritters, cream of tomato soup, salad with Thousand Island dressing, and of course, coffee and ice cream. Mr. Kentner boasted an entrepreneurial heart, and also offered reel projection movies for his patrons. With the advent of WWII he put in slot and pinball machines to take the stress of war off servicemen's shoulders. His daughter, Lorna "Bee" Kentner, also played the organ to accompany dancing.

The Twin Inns were a popular tourist spot for automobile travelers from Los Angeles and San Diego in the 1920s. This intrigue was also improved by Mr. Kentner's dedication to serving meals at all hours of the night. Prohibition also drove travelers, including Hollywood celebrities, south to the inns. Interestingly, a "speakeasy" existed in the basement.

The increase of tourists resulted in the expansion of the building. Mr. Kentner constructed the massive octagonal dining room around 1920. It became the town banquet hall, where weddings, anniversaries, the Marine Corps Ball, high school proms, etc., took place through the passing years. Also included was the addition of a rotunda in 1922. Town meetings took place in the rooms situated below the dining room. In 1936, the lobby and front rooms were also remodeled to provide for additional space. Surely, the Kentner family directly contributed to the overall success of the Twin Inns, serving as the social hub of the Carlsbad community.

In April 1984, the Kentner family sold the historic twin homes and all its land to Bob Burke. In 1985, the new proprietors changed its name to Neimans and developed the adjacent shopping area known as the Carlsbad Village Fair. In 2003, Neimans closed and was re-labeled the Ocean House. It served as a bar and nightclub until 2013. In November of the latter year Chef Robert Ruiz established his restaurant at the landmark location. The Land and Water Company was reinstituted inside its quarters, with the property being restored back to its original days. Today, the building offers one-of-a-kind California cuisine with French, Hawaiian, and Japanese influences to San Diego's northern areas.

With all of its historical significance, it is no wonder the Twin Inns also boast rumors of ghostly inhabitants. Many say that various spiritual energies exist inside its walls. Apparitional sightings of adults and children are seen on the historic property. The ethereal form of a woman peering out of one of the edifice's top buildings has been spotted. Employees have had experiences that they cannot explain; however, the spiritual residents are all thought to be friendly and curious.

Unexplained noises occur, and the sounds of invisible children are heard from time to time. Visitors have reported seeing a group of ghostly children playing games on the property. A delivery driver encountered one of the mansion's possible spirits when he ascended the stairs to an office on the top floor. He saw a young girl adorned in period attire sitting on the top of the stairs. Showing signs of intelligence as opposed to a residual imprint, she smiled at him when he passed by. As he delivered the package, he inquired to office staff as to who the little girl was. To his surprise, they told him that there were no girls around. Apparently this little child has been witnessed many times. Could these encounters be the spiritual residents of the Kentner family children?

It seems as though basements and ghosts go hand-in-hand. You guessed it: The Twin Inn's lowest dwelling room is also rumored to house ghostly energy. Whether this is due to power of suggestion or a true spiritual energy, many staff members report feeling uneasy here. It has often been rumored to be the location of illegal gambling in the 1920s. Intriguingly, employees have often found that bottles of liquor and soda cans turn up empty, even though the seals have not been penetrated. Could this be the result of some odd form of evaporation, or better yet, a prank by a mischievous employee?

Other occurrences have also been documented here. One staff member shared that the basement door slammed shut, but when he turned around, no one was there. An electrician reported that he felt some invisible presence tugging on his shirt while he was in the former chicken slaughter room. Sadly, he could not finish his work. Another person saw a woman in white in the exit area of the basement.

One of the prevailing theories for ghostly existence centers on the fact that water serves as a natural conductor of electricity. Since ghosts and spirits are thought to be made out of electricity, then it is safe to assume that water would serve as a natural battery for them. Could this be one of the reasons why the Twin Inns and other Carlsbad noted sites claim to have paranormal activity? Also, since the Twin Inns were a popular tourist spot and the social hub of Carlsbad, it is no surprise that it boasts a haunted reputation. Many people from all walks of life experienced happiness here, so that emotion is forever imprinted on the grounds that held this historical mansion.

PART IX:
East County San Diego's Most Haunted

San Diego's eastern regions are more rural and countrified, but that does not automatically dismiss them from having ghostly occurrences. Perhaps the paranormal activity in this portion of the city – as well as any portion – shares its storied past through the ghosts and spirits that continue to reside in the present. As the bustling city life seems to slow down the more eastward you travel, maybe it allows a person to tap more into the spiritual phenomena, as there are fewer distractions. No matter where you stand in San Diego, the olden times do find their way of seeping through to the present.

Chapter 29: Buckman Springs

> A very delicate water, and the only water of its kind on the market that may be drunk with impunity before and after, or with meals. Counteracts the evil effects of over-indulgence in eating and drinking.
> –Claim on a bottle of Buckman Springs Lithia Water

Perhaps the only trace that Buckman Springs ever existed is the dilapidated ruins of the Amos Buckman family home, its bottling plant, and a once-thriving hotel. As you drive east on Interstate 8, you will see a sign that reads, "Buckman Springs." As you exit off the road, you will travel west toward Buckman Springs Road, which will lead you right to the spot that was once a popular stop-off for stagecoaches and ten-mule wagons.

Buckman Springs was founded by Amos Buckman, who traveled to California from Vermont in 1853. Originally set up in Napa Valley, he hoped to establish springs that resembled the admired Saratoga Springs in upstate New York. He and his wife, Frances, relocated to San Diego after a stay-over in San Luis Obispo. They had four children: Emily (Emma), Hattie, Mary (Mamie), and Winifred (Winnie). Having arrived in the city in 1871, the couple purchased a house at Front and B Streets in 1872. While employed as a carpenter, he heard about the mineral springs in San Diego's eastern county, so he moved to the countrified setting approximately fifty miles east of the city.

In 1881, Amos was bestowed a 160-acre homestead in an area known as Indian Springs. Prior to the Buckman's ownership of the land, a Native American family resided there for many years. Here he constructed an eating house, cabins, and a hotel. Visitors traveling from Arizona to San Diego frequently stopped at the location after maneuvering through the mountains. One of the area's biggest attractions was the naturally carbonated water from the springs, possessing a substantial amount of silica, iron, and salt.

For more than fifty years, San Diego residents visited for two or three days to consume the bubbly water known to cure various ailments, such as dropsy (soft tissue swelling), bladder issues, rheumatism, stomach and liver disorders, and gastritis. The water also functioned as a mild laxative. Additionally, the spring water was listed as a hangover cure. The lithia water was bottled and sold locally for several years.

Mr. Buckman had wanted to develop a resort; however, his business struggled simply due to its rural location and the water's high iron content, which coated the bottles with a metallic orange hue. Unfortunately, this made the water less tempting to consume. At seventy-eight years old, Amos passed away on March 25, 1898. He was laid to rest at the springs that bore his name. Somewhat hidden, his headstone still remains. Apparently, Amos requested to be buried here as a way to always survey his property.

Winifred, one of Amos's children, inherited the land with the bottling works and hotel. She eventually added on to the business by incorporating a café and service station. In addition to selling the prized spring water she also sold flavored soda pop. In 1884, Winifred married Bruce Lee Casbere, a stage driver for the Butterfield "Jackass Mail" Line who used to stop over in Buckman Springs to water his horses. The couple commenced their married life at their cattle ranch in Cottonwood Valley, right next door to Buckman Springs. They had five children: Bruce, Hattie, Lotus, Arnie, and Arthur. The children lived on the land and attended school. The couple eventually divorced, and Winifred and the children ran the enterprise well into the 1940s. The business lasted until the passing of Winifred in 1946. Sadly, her children had trouble agreeing on ways to divide the property, so the industry ended with its land being sold.

Strange occurrences abound for the Buckman Springs back country. Whether these happenings are residual imprints from years ago or lingering intelligent spiritual energies remains a mystery. Perhaps ghostly vibrations from the land's Native American residents permeate the present. Could it be possible that the ongoing production of lithia water somehow created an eternal charge for paranormal energy? This question is postulated specifically due to the theory that ghosts and spirits are possibly made of electricity and water serves as a conductor.

There are weird events near Amos Buckman's grave site. Some people report hearing disembodied whispers and voices near his marker. Others have documented hearing footsteps maneuvering through the shrubs. I talked with a visitor who even reported seeing a male apparition materialize right in front of the burial location.

The bottling plant also boasts strange activity, and I am not just referring to transient alcoholic drinking fests. The San Diego Paranormal Research Society conducted a nighttime investigation of the former bottling facility, as well as the Buckman homestead ruins. While commencing the evening with a vigil to get a feel for the area we heard phantom footsteps walking around behind the former factory. These were rhythmic as opposed to intermittent. As we visually surveyed the area, one former team researcher announced that she saw an apparition of a Native American person. Intriguingly, when we went back during the daytime we noticed several *morteros* carved in the rocks, which were used by native peoples to grind nuts and seeds.

As the night waved on, we decided to visit the old ruins of the Buckman residence. All that exists now are the derelict remains of a home that once was. One of the last few pieces still standing is the fireplace, where we commenced our EVP session. During this time we asked the Buckman family questions pertaining to the history of their land and business affairs. While we did not capture any clear responses, we did note disembodied vocalizations occasionally coming through during our audio experiment. One investigator even recalled hearing the phantom sounds of children emanating as if they were standing right next to her. Are these youthful voices actually residual imprints from when the Buckman children lived on the property?

When thinking about the reasons behind some of the spiritual energy in Campo, you can't help but look into the residual occurrences left over from Camp Lockett. Campo is very close in proximity to Buckman Springs. Constructed as a United States Army military base in Campo, California, it has historical affiliations with the Buffalo Soldiers due to the 10th and 28th Cavalry Regiments that were garrisoned there during the Second World War. It has been reported that in the old barracks people can hear the phantom sounds of footsteps and smell phantom scents of pipe smoke. Even though there is a small distance between Buckman Springs and Camp Lockett, is it possible that the spiritual inhabitants of both locations intertwine with each other from time to time?

Chapter 30: Proctor Valley Road

Proctor Valley Road, about ten miles east of Bonita, is infamous for its fabled urban legends and ghost stories. The road is in desolate wilderness and connects Chula Vista to Jamul.

Ghost stories abound for this lonely dirt road. Tales include a cryptozoological ape-like beast, screaming banshees, and apparitions of hitchhikers. Some even claim that a phantom car will eerily tail you as you drive down the road. Some people have even reported vehicular mechanical breakdowns.

Many years ago, ranchers noticed that their cattle disappeared and were later discovered completely mutilated. This leaves many of us pondering whether alien activity and subsequent UFO visitations have occurred. Is there something that remains elusively hidden and mysterious in this area?

Many people have claimed to see the beast, also known as San Diego's Bigfoot. Some describe it as resembling the Mothman, whereas others describe it as looking like a gargantuan cow-like creature. A local psychiatrist chronicled his account of this mysterious being. He relayed that he saw a six- or seven-foot-tall hairy beast joined by two tiny creatures. In addition to making a sixteen-inch-long and eight-inch-wide footprint plaster cast, the medical doctor also documented hearing weird sounds near the vicinity of his home. Campers and other residents corroborate the psychiatrist's sightings of the monster.

One of the most intriguing urban legends has to do with a teenage couple's experiences while venturing on this abandoned nightmare of a road. According to myth, the two love birds parked their car along Proctor Valley Road; upon leaving this land of mystery their automobile suddenly broke down. The boyfriend got out of the vehicle to investigate the issue but was never heard from again. The girlfriend, riddled with heart-pounding fright, willingly remained inside the car as she heard scratching noises throughout the long night. Police located her the following day; however, her significant other's lifeless body was found hanging by a tree. Apparently, those eerie scratching sounds just happened to be from his hands as they touched on the car. Is this story the product of make believe or fabrication? Or is there some hard-to-believe truth associated with it? In my opinion, it sounds a little bit too ridiculous to be entirely true.

Let us next take a peek at the once-existent Haven Bakery at the eastern end of Proctor Valley Road in Jamul. Again, according to legend, the owner of the bakery returned from a business trip to find his young daughter lifelessly hanging by her neck in the basement. The dad then went mad and murdered the entire bakery staff and stacked their remains in the restroom prior to taking his own life. Prior to the bakery's demolition in 2008, it was reputed to be quite paranormally active, with the little girl's earthbound ghost haunting the basement where she allegedly breathed her last living breath.

Well, as it turns out, the true story held that a young girl accidentally fell down the basement steps and later succumbed at a local hospital. Apparently, a Walgreens stands in the exact spot where the Haven Bakery once resided. To date, I do not know of any Walgreens employee that has experienced any ghostly activity. Perhaps some people have had experiences but have not reported the incidences.

In addition to the aforementioned screaming banshee and ghostly hitchhiker, other phenomena have made their marks on the storied gravel road known as Proctor Valley. The ghost of a homeless man and a flying ball of fire have been said to manifest. More recently, the Chupacabra has also joined the Proctor Valley Road party of mystery. These cryptozoological creatures are said to mutilate animals in the middle of the night.

When you apply a good dose of common sense, it is hard to fathom the believability of these seemingly preposterous legends. Yes, while there may be residual ethereal energies of Native Americans or other settlers, these urban myths have most likely been fabricated and altered over time for the sheer purpose of establishing mystery, fear, and suspense.

Could there be a psychokinetic cause or made-up thought projection taking its own life form? In other words, if so many people believe that these legends are true, perhaps they enter our own reality as just that. For the most part, I believe that this barren stretch of land in the southeast part of San Diego's country has been exploited and duped by a series of fabled, nonsensical stories.

Chapter 31: Santee Edgemoor Barn

The Santee Edgemoor Barn is full of paranormal energy.

The City of Santee began as a minute backcountry community in the latter portion of the nineteenth century. It eventually developed into a diverse and versatile portion of one of San Diego's eastern cities. The Spanish parceled the area of Santee into land grants and divided them among Spanish military personnel as reimbursement for their services.

Native Americans settled in San Diego County some 12,000 years ago. The terrain surrounding Santee consisted of a portion of the El Cajon Valley. The area was primarily utilized for the Mission San Diego de Alcalá's grazing livestock. In 1845, Maria Antonia Estudillo de Pedrorena acquired a land grant of 48,799 acres from the Mexican government in payment of a small debt allocated to her late husband. This sprawling land would later become known as El Cajon, Lakeside, Santee, and Flinn Springs.

As the years went on, the region was eventually sold to American settlers, including its founding father, George A. Cowles. Mr. Cowles purchased 4,000 acres in 1877, to build his vineyards. Previously known as Cowleston, the town of Santee was connected to the Cuyamaca Railroad at Cowles Station. Jennie Cowles married realtor and assessor Milton Santee after Mr. Cowles's demise in 1887. In 1885, Hosmer P. McKoon traveled to the region and purchased 9,543 acres known as Fanita Ranch. The town then became known as Santee in 1893.

In 1898, the Scripps family took over management of the ranch, turning it into a country resort, as well as a cattle ranch. The federal government attained 2,300 acres of Fanita Ranch during World War II and used it as a military training ground. As the years progressed, portions of this ranch were sold to new settlers to the area. In fact, the region's populace increased from less than 2,000 inhabitants in 1950 to 25,750 in 1970. Incorporated in 1980, the City of Santee continues to thrive as a residential and commercial region.

One of the most frequently talked about historical locations in Santee is the former Edgemoor Hospital and dairy farm. Chicago-based businessman John H. Dupee had many new buildings constructed on the Edgemoor ranch between 1913 and 1915. When passenger rail service reached Santee in 1915, Edgemoor then became an attractive tourist spot for San Diegans.

For $85,000, Mr. Dupee purchased the Williamson's 500-acre farm for his son, Walter Hamlin Dupee. He was dedicated to running the biggest dairy farm in the area, with it eventually becoming one of the most influential at the time. The farm helped to educate people on cattle rearing and dairy production, bringing national awareness and appreciation to the region's flourishing dairy industry. Santee then became known internationally for its esteemed polo ponies.

During the late Colonial period America relegated society's deprived, helpless, and oppressed individuals to "almshouses," more commonly known as poor farms. By the late 1920s, in California, approximately fifty county hospitals and poor farms existed. Eventually, they were phased out or became facilities for elderly care. Many of these poor houses became extinct by the mid-1950s, but continued as publicly funded nursing homes for the elderly and infirm. In fact, as the shift went from farming to more legitimate medical care in the latter 1940s, the poor farm era at Edgemoor eventually came to a halt. Edgemoor commenced the 1950s, with a new concentration on skilled nursing and rehabilitative treatment of elderly individuals.

The Edgemoor Farm and San Diego County Home for the Aged and Indigent was founded in Santee during 1923. In the same year, the County of San Diego utilized around 500 acres in Santee for the County Poor Farm. A brand-new patient facility was constructed in 1955, known as the Edgemoor Geriatric Hospital. The 375-acre facility catered to underprivileged people, treating those with tuberculosis and polio, as well as psychiatric conditions. Later on it cared for poor, homeless, and geriatric individuals.

Edgemoor has endured one hundred years of compassionately caring for individuals with specialized needs. Today, many people suffering from severe illnesses and/or injuries come to its facilities to receive treatment. Its hospital functions in combination with the County of San Diego Psychiatric Hospital. Some of its patients, ranging from eighteen to eighty years old, may be dealing with Huntington's disease, AIDS, or traumatic injuries. A personal physician coordinates treatment for the entire duration of patients' stays.

The modern, state-of-the art Edgemoor facility is a prime example of centralized patient care, where each department works in unison to offer the best treatment for each individual patient. Today it offers skilled nursing and long term care for individuals. With 168,000 square feet, the facility is divided into six neighborhoods with thirty-two beds each. In addition to medical care, patients can participate in various therapeutic care activities, such as arts and crafts, cooking and baking, exercise, ceramics, and religion.

Perhaps the ranch's most famous edifice was completed on July 19, 1913, serving as a substantial barn utilized for Dupee's award-winning team of bulls. It would later be referred to as the Polo Barn, after he initiated the nurturing of polo ponies. Mr. Dupee also built a number of other buildings, including a residence, three dairy farms, and a gardener's shop. After extensive renovation in 1955, Edgemoor Hospital utilized the structure as a central supply warehouse and storage facility until February 2007.

As of that year, the Santee Historical Society moved its organization into the Edgemoor Barn. It was eventually listed on the National Register of Historic Places by the United States Department of the Interior in 1985. Today, the remarkable structure stands in its original location, known as the last remaining Dupee-period original building. One of the oldest buildings in Santee, the barn represents a time when farming was crucial to San Diego's culture and economy.

The Edgemoor facilities are perhaps Santee's most well-known historical sites. We know that history and the paranormal go hand-in-hand; they are best friends with a dear kinship. Furthermore, hospital and medical facilities are on the list of places most commonly associated with supernatural energy. For one, human suffering and pain somehow attract spiritual energy. For years people have reported strange activity occurring throughout the Edgemoor premises, including the exact barn that now houses the Santee Historical Society.

Employees have reported various paranormal goings on at the old Edgemoor grounds. Some have witnessed patient call lights turning on when no patients were in their beds, to televisions and other electronics operating of their own volition. Volunteers for the historical society have documented ghostly occurrences inside the barn, including disembodied voices, apparitional sightings, and phantom footsteps. Electronic Voice Phenomena (alleged spirit voices not heard at the time of actual recording) have been consistently captured. Some residents in neighboring homes also document strange encounters. Whether the Edgemoor premises are actually haunted remains to be seen, but there seems to be some indication of its paranormal energy.

One historical society member captured what looked like a UFO hovering directly above the barn while she was taking photographs. Air fields near the facility were not able to offer a logical explanation. Intriguingly, the photographer reported that her camera malfunctioned right after she snapped the picture. If indeed this was the capture of a genuine UFO, then it makes me wonder if there is something about the land itself that is captivating to foreign life species. If there is, then maybe this could also have something to do with the ghostly energy inhabiting the premises. Alien life may be specifically attracted to San Diego due to its military significance, as many other people have witnessed strange objects in its skies. I have personally witnessed possible UFO activity in "America's Finest City" on two occasions, having directly spotted the entity above the community I reside in.

Afterword

I have spent much of my thirty-seven years residing in San Diego, California. This southernmost California location has provided me with rich opportunities to explore my own path and destiny while in this mortal realm. This is the place on the national map where I have traveled down a path of individual discovery and have realized my genuine love of paranormal research and writing. San Diego is intertwined in my soul, so much so that no matter what the future has in store, I will always consider it my hometown.

Just like the Pacific Ocean waves that come and go, San Diego's history includes several notable people that have made lasting impressions on the city, thus shaping and being a part of what it is today. Even though the majority of these folks have passed on, the buildings they created and/or resided in remain a part of an ongoing quest by continuing to share their legacy with people of all ages.

Perhaps history is the most vital contributor to either intelligent or residual paranormal energy. It helps to highlight spiritual activity's way of telling a story of past times; in many ways, those previous days and years of long ago assist in shaping our present. Many individuals travel to San Diego throughout the year to partake in activities galore, exquisite weather, and serene beauty. It is my hope that when you visit this rich, historical city, you give thanks to its founding fathers and contributors, as they have ultimately created the rich historical tapestry known in "America's Finest City."

Writing this book is my own unique way of thanking San Diego and its pioneers for all that they have done. *San Diego's Most Haunted* is written to bridge the history and supernatural happenings of many of the city's most notable hauntings. The paranormal activity at these legendary sites exists to nostalgically educate current residents and visitors of bygone eras. One really cannot have an appreciation for ghostly occurrences without an understanding and indebtedness to history. In my opinion, each spiritual encounter is a historic site's way of keeping its past alive in the present.

Along with the San Diego Paranormal Research Society and other paranormal investigation teams, I have had the opportunity to conduct in-depth research at many of the locations mentioned in this book. By encountering the ethereal presences of some of the city's past revolutionary residents and early pioneers, it has given me an even greater admiration for the history of this celebrated city. Additionally, it has further sparked my intrigue in and dedication to continuing the historical research of this famous metropolis.

PART X:
Appendices and Resources

Signs that Your Location May Be Haunted: What to Look For

It is imperative to always try and find a logical explanation for the types of odd activity occurring at your location. If you have exhausted all measures in trying to determine the cause, only then are you left with the possibility of paranormal activity. Try not to jump to the conclusion that what you are experiencing is due to something supernatural. Apply the fields of medicine, psychology, engineering, etc., in trying to explain what is going on. Remember, most reported types of anomalous activity have a natural explanation. Also, keep in mind that just because a site may have paranormal occurrences, it does not necessarily make it a "haunted" location. Usually with haunted locales there has to be some sort of spirit connection to the property.

History: History and the paranormal share a deep kinship, so locations with noted historical events are more capable of having paranormal activity. This includes any prior deaths, burial grounds, nearby cemeteries, or any other fatal catastrophes occurring on or near the property. For private residences, it is important to research your home's history and prior occupants.

Unexplainable Noises and Sounds: Sounds, including footsteps, knocks, banging, rapping, scratching, etc., can all be indicative that something strange is going on. Sometimes these noises can be subtle, and other times they can be quite loud. Always check your home's foundation and make sure there are no problems with it. Older homes produce more of these types of eerie sounds. Make sure you do not have uninvited furry guests in your home, either.

Psychokinetic Energy (PK): In the movies we all have seen cabinet doors or other pieces of furniture open and close, or move of their own volition. Many people refer to this as poltergeist activity. Usually a person walks into a space and notices this, as opposed to seeing it happen. If there is no reason for it, it may be due to a psychokinetic influence, where the mind can somehow move an object. Normally, this PK activity is seen in pre-pubescent or pubescent teenagers, or those experiencing high emotional states. Again, when this does occur, check to see if it is a foundation problem, or if there is some other issue causing the events.

Plumbing Issues: Some people witness water faucets and/or showers turning on or off of their own volition. If this happens always have a plumber come inspect the problem. Chances are there is a natural explanation for the issue. There is a theory that spiritual energy holds electrical charges. Water is a natural conductor for electricity, so keep in mind that some places on or near lots of water may be more capable of attracting paranormal energy.

Electrical Issues: Many people report lights or other devices turning on and off by themselves. Most often there is a natural explanation for this. Again, always have an electrician come and check the problem. Make sure that your television's automatic timer is not the root cause of it turning on or off by itself. Another recommendation is to test each outlet in your home with a wire receptacle tester. It is theorized that the electromagnetic field may influence and/or cause paranormal activity. Places that have a lot of electrical devices may experience more strange occurrences.

Unexplainable Shadows: Many odd shadow sightings have natural explanations. However, if the shadow form exhibits some form of intelligence and/or appears at the same time every day, then you may be dealing with something different. If you notice the anomaly out of your peripheral vision and see that it resembles grey and/or black humanoid shapes, you may be dealing with some form of paranormal energy. Shadow energies are most often residual in nature, similar to a psychic imprint on the environment. Keep a log of your sightings and note the characteristics and location where you witness them.

There is another type of shadow figure anomaly discussed in the paranormal research field known as the "Classic Shadow Person." These types are thought to be non-human energies that have somehow traveled through a wormhole into our dimension with the sole purpose of observing the living. Their classic characteristics are either very short or very tall black humanoid figures. They are sometimes seen adorned in a cape and wide-brimmed hat. They usually appear and disappear very quickly and move at lightning speed. Some researchers believe that they originate from alien species.

The Apport Theory: If you notice items appearing in your location from out of nowhere, you may be dealing with apport phenomena. Basically, this is the paranormal transference of one article from one place to another. Typically this is common with very old, antique items.

Antiques: Speaking about antiques, locations that have a lot of vintage items are said to experience paranormal phenomena. It is theorized that some ghosts and spirits may be attached to a certain object or location, or the antique may hold memories and energy from the past, sometimes attracting the spirit world. If you purchase an antique item, there are ways to possibly cleanse and/or possibly remove any attached energy. Certain incense and crystal varieties can be helpful with this, along with positive affirmations.

Apparition Sightings: Apparitions are thought to be the grail of all paranormal activity. If you have seen one at your location it may be residual or intelligent, or at times a combination of both. Remember, with residual activity it has no intelligence and does not interact with the living. With intelligent activity, ghosts and/or spirits can communicate with the living and interact with them. There are many classifications of ghosts and spirits. I recommend reading *The Case for Ghosts: An Objective Look at the Paranormal* by Allan Danelek. It is a fascinating read that covers the various types of ghosts and spirits. Some people have seen a spirit double of themselves or another person. Known as a doppleganger, these occurrences tend to take place around times of stress or directly before or after someone's death. If you have constant feelings of being watched by unseen eyes then you may have a spiritual guest at your location. Frankincense, musk, and sandalwood are great to use for calming and purifying an area.

Odd Animal Behavior: If you witness your animals behaving in strange ways of course have them evaluated by their veterinarian. However, certain animals have a keen ability to sense spiritual energy, especially dogs, cats, and horses. Common animal behavior during a paranormal event includes: 1) the animal may sit and stare at a certain spot for a long time; 2) fear of going into a certain area; 3) acting as though they are communicating with an unseen presence; and 4) barking, meowing, or crying for no reason. If your furry friend is looking at something that you cannot see, study their eye movements. Our beloved pets have heightened senses and can see and hear better than we can. This is one of the reasons why some paranormal researchers utilize animals during their investigations.

Hypnagogia: The transitional phase from being awake to falling asleep is known as hypnagogia. In this state people can experience sleep paralysis, as well as auditory, visual, and olfactory hallucinations. It is thought that there is sometimes a connection between hypnagogia and communication with spiritual activity.

Tulpa and Thought Projection: A tulpa is basically like a thought projection. It is created by a living person, and due to its psychokinetic properties it can be projected on to the environment. Once this occurs it can start to develop its own personality traits. Some researchers theorize that some people's thought projections may be misconstrued for a genuine spiritual entity. It is also theorized that some malevolent and negative energy are the result of one's own personal baggage somehow being projected on to the environment, generating its own life force.

What to Include in a Case Report: Investigation Case Report Guidelines

1. Review all photographs, audio, ITC, video, environmental meter findings, etc.

2. Document personal experiences as they happen while conducting the investigation. Make copies of any and all data logs.

3. Even if you do not have any evidence to submit, a report still needs to be sent documenting personal experiences or intuitive impressions. This is very important.

4. All reports need to have the following pieces of information:

- Environmental conditions (weather, humidity, solar storm info, moon phases, etc.)
- Team member partnered with
- Equipment used during preliminary investigation and actual investigation
- Experiments conducted throughout investigation
- Paranormal vigil log
- Personal experiences and/or intuitive impressions
- Duties during the investigation
- Start time and end time of your experiments
- Evidence summary sheet (see below)

5. Evidence summary sheets for photographs, audio, and video.

These need to be numbered and include the file name and exact time the photograph, video clip, or audio clip was captured. Include "cue" times as well so it is easier for clients to zero in on when the anomaly occurs. There also needs to be a small descriptive summary of findings for each piece of evidence submitted.

SDPRS Classes and Lectures

Classes

Introduction to Paranormal Investigating: This class is an introduction to paranormal investigating and explains some prevalent theories of what ghosts and hauntings are. This class explores common theories of what constitutes ghosts and hauntings and terminology related to paranormal investigating. Furthermore, this class discusses techniques and methods of conducting a paranormal investigation, including equipment, theories, and methodologies.

The Spirit of Paranormal Research: This class is basically "Paranormal Research 101," as it goes over important aspects of paranormal research, including proper protocol and standard operating procedures needed for a successful research experience. It actually serves as a motivator for anyone interested in learning more about ghost research and investigation. The SDPRS team discusses the desired attributes and traits of a solid researcher while also addressing not-so-desired traits seen in the field today. Topics include: the tent poles and foundations of a solid researcher and investigative team, methodology, evidence review techniques, equipment practice, grounding and meditation techniques, and professional development.

Electronic Voice Phenomena: What is it? How to Conduct an EVP Session: This class discusses a brief history of Electronic Voice Phenomena, as well as offering helpful hints and suggestions for conducting an EVP session. SDPRS will talk about the methods it uses when conducting an EVP session. Also included are protocols and suggestions for conducting EVP and ITC work at a location.

Lectures

The Haunted Queen of the Seas: The Living Legend of the RMS Queen Mary: Offered by Nicole Strickland, this lecture offers a brief history of the RMS *Queen Mary* from its construction and relentless career on the high seas all the way up to its current golden age in retirement. Furthermore, this presentation discusses the common paranormal activity that occurs throughout the ship, including prevalent theories for the ship's hauntings. Nicole will share some of the possible paranormal documentation she has obtained on the ship.

Children and the Paranormal: Join SDPRS member Nicole Strickland as she combines her experience with children and her educational background in educational counseling with that of the paranormal. This class explores the stages of child development, and how children might be affected by paranormal phenomena during each stage of development. This class will discuss the common signs that a child is being affected by paranormal activity and will offer suggestions for parents, guardians, and even paranormal investigators for helping a child and his/her family who are dealing with a possible haunting.

Glossary of Paranormal Terminology

Reference: Ghost PRO (Paranormal Research Organization)

Agent: A living person thought to be the cause of paranormal phenomena. This person may increase activity or be the entire cause of the activity.

Amulet: An object that is theorized to bring good luck and protection from certain spiritual energies.

Anomaly: A series of events that do not follow a chain of logic; unusual activity that cannot be scientifically explained.

Apparition: Another term for a ghost. The witness usually describes an apparition as having a distinct form and/or distinct features. Apparitions can appear in both residual and intelligent hauntings.

Apport: A physical object that can appear suddenly. It is thought that the apported items are somehow related to the deceased and the appearance of these items is the deceased's effort to make contact.

Audible Voice Phenomena (AVP): An AVP is a disembodied voice that is heard at the time of recording and is also captured on a recording device.

Automatic Writing: An antique method used by spiritual mediums to contact the afterlife. During automatic writing, it has been thought that spirits can control and cause the medium to produce unconscious writing on paper. It is not as commonly practiced today.

Banshee: Another term for a death omen or entity that becomes attached to certain individuals.

Case Study: A thorough examination of a location for alleged paranormal activity.

Channeling: A technique where intuitively inclined individuals pass information obtained from a spiritual entity to others.

Clairaudience: The ability to gain spirit information via vocalizations, whispers, and other auditory impressions.

Clairsentience: The ability to perceive and experience the emotions of others without using the five senses.

Clairvoyance: The ability to see what appears invisible to most people. People who claim to be clairvoyant say that they can see ghosts.

Collective Apparition: This occurs when more than one witness sees the same exact ghost.

Crisis Apparition: An apparition that is seen close to the time of his/her death. This can also apply to situations where an apparition appears to a loved one around the time of his/her death.

Debunking: To find a logical or natural explanation for alleged paranormal activity.

Dematerialization: To see the disappearance or de-manifestation of an entity.

Doppelganger: The apparition or mirror image of a still living person. Some believe that these are associated with negativity, or even death.

Dowsing Rod: A tool used to locate water, certain objects, or energy fields; also serves as an adjunct tool in paranormal investigations, especially during a "yes" and "no" Q&A session.

Earthbound: A word to describe a ghost who has not been able to cross over to the other side and is thereby stuck in the mortal realm.

Ectoplasm: An ethereal substance associated with spirit manifestation that is often photographed as a whitish mist or vortex.

Electromagnetic Field (EMF): A natural or man-made energy field surrounding all things.

Electronic Voice Phenomena (EVP): The capturing of voices and/or sounds on tape or recorder that are not heard at the time the recording took place. These voices/sounds are heard upon playback of tape or recorder. There are four classes to EVP: Class A, Class B, Class C, and Class R.

Elementals: Earthbound spirits; some believe that elementals are associated with negative entities.

Empath: See Clairsentience.

Entity: Something that has a separate, distinct existence, not necessarily material in nature.

Extra Sensory Perception (ESP): Perceiving or communicating without using the five senses.

False Awakening: An event where people think they are awake but are actually asleep in a dream state.

Frank's Box: A type of spirit box that works by continuously scanning AM and FM radio bands. It is theorized that spiritual energies can utilize and manipulate the electronic frequencies of the device to form words, thereby allowing real-time communication with the living.

Ghost: The most widely used term to describe paranormal entities. It is the disembodied form of a human being, animal, or object.

Haunting: Continuous paranormal activity that takes place at a certain location that can last for a very short time or a very long time. For a haunting to take place, there has to be some historical tie or connection to the property.

Hypnagogia: A state where a person is in between a sleep and awake state; commonly associated with sleep paralysis.

Instrumental Trans Communication (ITC): Alleged spirit voices that can come through modern technology in real-time. Real-time communication between the living and departed via various electronic devices.

Intelligent Haunting: A haunting where the deceased makes an intelligent effort to communicate with the living.

Intuitive Inclined Individual: A person with psychic abilities who can sense the presence of spiritual energy.

Matrixing: To make form or shape out of something that is not there. This is commonly seen in photographs and/or on video where people think they may see a face or shape, but it is nothing more than the witness' imagination at work.

Orbs: Circular and opaque objects that are caught on still photographs and on film. Some believe these orbs consist of spiritual energy or paranormal phenomena.

Paranormal: Not of the normal realm; also describes events or situations that are out of our realm of understanding. Events or situations that are unexplainable.

Pareidolia: A common psychological phenomenon where the brain organizes a random stimulus into an organized pattern. Also known as matrixing, an example is seeing faces or animals in the clouds.

Percipient: An individual who sees or perceives an apparition.

Poltergeist: Literally the German word for "noisy ghost." In cases involving poltergeist phenomena, people describe objects moving about of their own volition. However, many paranormal researchers believe that a human agent is the cause of poltergeist events. This person is usually a pubescent female and/or someone going through emotional distress.

Precognition: The ability to conceive of an event prior to its actual occurrence, especially via ESP.

Psychic: A person who is thought to have sensitivity beyond what normal people have. A person with this ability can see, hear, and feel what many people cannot.

Psychokinesis (PK): The ability of the mind to influence the movement of an object, such as in cases involving poltergeist phenomena.

Psychometry: The ability to gain information about a person or place simply by touching an associated object.

Reciprocal Apparition: An unusual event when both the agent and percipient are able to visualize and respond to each other.

Remote Viewing: Via ESP, a procedure where a psychic or intuitive can become aware of a person, place, or events from another location.

Residual Haunting: A residual haunting is similar to a psychic imprint left on the environment. Events that were so important or filled with a lot of emotion leave an imprint on the environment, and thus keep replaying themselves over and over. A phantom battle scene at Gettysburg can be an example of a residual haunting.

Retrocognition: When a person finds himself or herself in the past and becomes aware of past events that they had no prior knowledge of.

Séance: A procedure for trying to communicate with the deceased. In a séance, individuals will be situated around a table and a person, usually a psychic, will lead the session and contact the deceased.

Shadow Figure: A partial apparition that appears in dark grey or black tones. Some researchers believe that apparitions that are only partially manifested appear as humanoid shadows. The Classic Shadow Person is a bit different, however, and is theorized to be a form of alien species with the sole purpose of observing and studying the living. These shadow people appear as very tall or short, often adorned in a cape and wide-brimmed hat. They move extremely fast and are often seen peering around corners.

Sleep Paralysis: See Hynagogia.

Specter: Another word for a ghost.

Spirit: A ghost or discarnate entity. Many people use ghost and spirit interchangeably, but some researchers believe that spirits differ from a ghost, in that a spirit has the ability to travel back and forth from this world to the afterlife with free will.

Spirit Photography: Photography that contains some form of paranormal phenomena that cannot be explained by natural means. Many paranormal investigators specialize in spirit photography in hopes of capturing paranormal phenomena on film.

Supernatural: Relating to existence outside the natural world.

Talisman: See Amulet.

Telekinesis: The movement of objects by paranormal means.

Telepathy: The ability to tap into the mind of someone else; when two minds are linked as one. Communication between the living and deceased can be telepathic.

Tulpas: Thought projections that take on their own life forms; spirit energies being created from the human mind.

Vigil: In paranormal research, a vigil is described as observing a particular environment for a set period of time while utilizing various electronic instruments and intuitive capabilities.

Vortex: A photographic anomaly depicting a rope-like substance of ghosts, orbs, or gateways traveling through a wormhole; unexplainable by scientific means.

White Noise: The static sounds that are utilized as background noise to help produce spirit voices on tape during an EVP session.

Bibliography

Allbeury, Joseph. *Russian Cobra Foxtrot-Class Submarine*. Australia: Jasper Communications, 1998 & 2002.

Arnold, Craig. *Euterpe: Diaries, Letters and Logs of the "Star of India" as a British Emigrant Ship*. San Diego, CA: The Maritime Museum Association of San Diego (1988): 10–13, 108–109.

Bradley, Donna. *Native Americans of San Diego County*. San Diego, CA: Arcadia Publishing, 2009.

Bugbee, Carrico Susan and Kathleen Flanigan. *San Diego's Gaslamp Quarter: Then and Now*. San Diego, CA: Tecolote Publications, iii, v, vi, vii, pg. 24–25.

Carrico, Richard. *San Diego's Spirits: Ghosts and Hauntings in America's Southwest Corner.* California: Susan Carrico, 1991.

Chamberlin, Eugene K. *San Diego Presidio Site*. San Diego, CA: Presidio Park, Old Town, 1992, pg 8–13.

Crawford, Hubbard Leslie. *Images of America: Coronado*. San Diego, CA: Arcadia Publishing, 2011, pg. 7–11, 20–22, 27, 29, 32, 59–61, 73–74, 77, 113.

Crawford, Kathleen A. "Exploring San Diego's Past: Fifty Years of the Journal of San Diego History." *The Journal of San Diego History*, 50 (2004): 67.

Crawford, Richard W. "Rancho Guajome: An Architectural Legacy." *The Journal of San Diego History*. Fall 1995. Volume 41. #4.

Danelek, Allan J. *A Case for Ghosts: An Objective Look at the Paranormal.* Woodbury, MN: Llewellyn Publications, 2006.

Donaldson, Milford Wayne. *Ferryboat* "Berkeley." San Diego, CA: San Diego Maritime Museum, 2000, pg. 1–14.

Dutton, Davis. *San Diego and the Back Country*. New York: Ballantine Comstock, 1972, 12–16.

Edgemoor Farm Historical Resources Evaluation Report. San Diego, CA: County of San Diego Department of General Service, 2008. pg. 1–27, 40–48, 69.

Edgemoor Hospital Patient Information. Santee, CA: A Division of Aging and Independent Services: A Health and Human Services Agency, 2004. pg. 1–2

El Campo Santo. San Diego, CA: Old Town, San Diego, 1994, pg. 8–10, 13, 29.

"El Fandango Restaurant" HauntedHouses.com, accessed October 9, 2016. http://hauntedhouses.com/states/ca/el_fandango.htm

"El Fandango Restaurant," *Weird California*, accessed October 21, 2016, http://www.weirdca.com/location.php?location=63

Engstrand, Iris H. W. "A Brief Sketch of San Diego's Military Presence: 1542–1945." *The Journal of San Diego History*. Winter-Spring 2014., Volume 60. #1 and 2.

Engstrand, Iris H. W. *Old Town San Diego, 1821–1874: A Brief History and Descriptive Guide to Historic Sites*. California: Alcalá Press, 1976, pg. 3–11, 16, 18, 24, 26.

Engstrand, Iris H. W. *Serra's San Diego: Father Junípero Serra and California's Beginners*. San Diego Historical Society, CA, 1982.

Ewing, Hanks Nancy. *Del Mar: Looking Back*. Del Mar, CA: The Del Mar History Foundation, 1988.

Fark, Bill. "Brief History of Escondido" accessed October 21, 2016, at http://www.escondidohistory.com.

"First Sight of Carlsbad." Carlsbad Historical Society, accessed October 21, 2016, at http://carlsbadhistoricalsociety.com/

"Glossary of Paranormal Terms." Ghost PRO (Paranormal Research Organization), accessed October 21, 2016, at http://ghostpro.org/glossary/glossary.html

Griswold del Castillo, Richard. "The U.S.-Mexican War in San Diego, 1846–1847." *The Journal of San Diego History*. Winter 2003. Volume 49. #1.

Harris, Michael. "El Campo Santo, Old Town San Diego, San Diego County, California." California Tombstone Project, February 23, 2007, accessed October 21, 2016, http://files.usgwarchives.net/ca/sandiego/cemeteries/elcampo-santo.txt

"History of Carlsbad." Carlsbad Historical Society, accessed October 21, 2016 at http://carlsbadhistoricalsociety.com/

"History." Elfin Forest Harmony Grove Town Council, accessed October 21, 2016, http://www.efhgtc.org/history.html

Hopkins, Harry C. *History of San Diego: Its Pueblo Lands and Water*. California: City Printing Company, 1929, pg. 23–25, 34–35, 43–51, 86, 96, 169.

Images of America: San Diego's Gaslamp Quarter. Charleston, SC: Arcadia Publishing, 2003, pg. 66–67.

Howard-Jones, Marje. *Seekers of the Spring: A History of Carlsbad*. Carlsbad, CA: Friends of the Carlsbad Library, 1982, pg. 1–3, 52–53, 76–80.

"Inquisition by Coroner's Jury." The Whaley House Museum, accessed October 9, 2016, http://whaleyhouse.org/coroner.htm

Jordan, Kathryn A. "Life Beyond Gold: A New Look at the History of Julian, California." *The Journal of San Diego History*. Spring 2008. Volume 54. #2.

Lamb, John. *San Diego Specters*. California: Sunbelt Publications, 1999.

Lawson, Gabriel. "The Role of Cemeteries in Historical Research: The Curious Case of Pioneer Park." *The Journal of San Diego History*. Winter–Spring 2011. Volume 57. #1 and 2.

LeMenager, Charles R. *Julian City and Cuyamaca Country: A History and Guide to the Past and Present*. San Diego, CA: Createspace Independent Publishing Platform, 2014, pg. 1–23, 37–58, 131–132, 140–146, 204, 216–217.

Lister, Priscilla. "Pioneer Park May Haunt You—at Least with its Stories," *San Diego Uptown News*, October 19, 2009, accessed October 21, 2016, http://sduptownnews.com/pioneer-park- may-haunt-you-at-least-with-its-stories/

"Lottiepedia Kate Morgan," Coronado Mystery, accessed November 1, 2017 at http://www.coronadomystery.com/lottiepedia/lottiepedia-kate-morgan.html

MacPhail, Elizabeth C. *The Story of New San Diego and its Founder Alonzo E. Horton*. San Diego, CA: Pioneer Printers, 1969, pg. 19–38.

McShane, Catherine Sister PhD. "The Estudillo Family." *The Journal of San Diego History*, Winter 1969. Volume 15. #1.

Meyer, Roy W. *History of the Santee Sioux: United States Indian Policy on Trial*. Nebraska: University of Nebraska, 1993.

Mills, James R. "San Diego: Where California Began." *San Diego History Center Quarterly*. San Diego, 1960. Volume VI. #1.

Moriarty, James R. "Father Serra and the Soldiers." *The Journal of San Diego History*. Summer 1967. Volume 13. #3.

Morrow, Thomas J. and William Sullivan. *Hotel del Coronado*. Coronado, CA: The Hotel Del Coronado, 1984, pg. 9, 10–23.

Moss, James E. "The Davis House." *The Journal of San Diego History*. Fall 1971. Volume 17. #4.

Pequegnat, Linda. *This Day in San Diego History*. California: Sunbelt Publications, 2009, pg. 9, 13–14, 43, 93, 108, 120 131, 150, 175, 180, 187, 201, 228, 242, 298, 350, 200, 230, 260, 342–343, 361.

Rand, Elizabeth H. and Joan C. Tucker. *San Diego and the Southland: Just the Facts: A Guide to Sightseeing*. San Diego, CA: Rand Editions/Tofua Press, 1984, pg. 8–9, 12–16.

Roll, Andrew F. *William Heath Davis and the Founding of American San Diego*. California: University of California Press, 1952.

San Diego: A California City. New York, NY: AMS Press, 1975, pg. 9, 17, 21–45, 72–74

Schiff, Matthew G. "Placing the Past in the Present: The Creation of Old Town San Diego State Historic Park." *The Journal of San Diego History*. Summer 2011. Volume 57. #3.

Schwartz, Henry. *Tales of Old Town*. San Diego, CA: Associated Creative Writers, 1980, pg. 8–11, 76–82.

Sharp, Dennis G. "Reconstructed Adobe: The Spanish Past in the Architectural Records of the San Diego Historical Society, 1907–1929." *Journal of San Diego History*. Summer-Fall 2003. Volume 49. #3 & 4.

Smith, Gifford Walter. *The Story of San Diego*. San Diego, CA: San Diego City Printing Company, 1892, pg. 96–101.

Smythe, William Ellsworth. *History of San Diego, 1542–1908*. San Diego, CA: History Co., 1907, pg 154–157, 164–167.

Strickland, Nicole. *Field Guide to Southern California Hauntings*. Chicago: Ghost Research Society Press, 2009, 35–37.

Strudwick, June A. "The Whaley House." *The Journal of San Diego History*. Spring 1960. Volume 6. #2.

Taylor, Troy. *Field Guide to Haunted Graveyards*. Illinois: Whitechapel Productions, 2003.

The Thomas Whaley House. San Diego, CA: Historical Shrine Foundation of San Diego County, 1960.

Walsh, Victor A. "The Casa and the Don: Juan Bandini's Quest for Homeland in Early San Diego." *The Journal of San Diego History*. Summer 2012. Volume 57. #1.

Westbrook, Devlin. "Ghost Tour and Haunted Grand Horton Hotel in Downtown San Diego." *San Diego Reader*, September 9, 2013. Accessed October 21, 2016. http://www.sandiegoreader.com/weblogs/devlins-corner/2013/sep/09/ghost-/tour-and-haunted-grand-horton-hotel-in-downt/

White, Gail. *Haunted San Diego: A Historic Guide to San Diego's Favorite Haunts*. California: Tecolote Publications, 1993.

Williams, Amy. "The Del Mar Racetrack: 75 Years of Turf and Surf." *The Journal of San Diego History*. Summer 2012. Volume 58. #3.

Acknowledgments

First of all, I want to give thanks to all the people of San Diego's bygone eras, as the city would not be what it is today without their relentless efforts.

Juan and Ysidora, et al., I want to thank you for the times we have spent together and for your contributions to the history of San Diego.

With much appreciation, I want to give thanks to all of the contributors to this book, as their individual portions all add something special. I am indebted to Marie Jones for writing the book's foreword.

I want to acknowledge all of my paranormal research colleagues for their encouragement. A special mention goes to San Diego Paranormal Research Society Co-Director Ali Schreiber for her tireless work and devotion to the team. Here's to many more memorable times.

Thank you to Rachel Greene, owner and lead editor for Penoaks Publishing, for her expertise with editing and formatting.

I am grateful for my Schiffer Publishing editor Dinah Roseberry, especially for her guidance and mentorship along the way.

Much gratitude goes to my family for your love, support, and encouragement. I love you all so much.

The author aboard the RMS *Queen Mary* for a book signing. She has written two books about the historic liner's history and paranormal happenings.

About the Author

Nicole Strickland currently resides in San Diego, California, and has been intrigued with the paranormal since childhood. She has studied the field for many years. She has been actively investigating historical landmarks, other businesses, and private residences for paranormal activity since the early 2000s, after a profound experience with the spirit of her beloved grandmother, Helen Lopinto.

Nicole is the founder and director of the well-respected San Diego Paranormal Research Society (SDPRS) and serves as the team's case manager. Nicole has also worked with various Southern California paranormal research teams prior to developing SDPRS in 2009. Additionally, Nicole serves as a California representative for the American Spectral Society and as a consultant to World Paranormal Investigations.

Other Books by Nicole

Nicole published her first book, *Field Guide to Southern California Hauntings*, in 2009. Her second book, *The Haunted Queen of the Seas: The Living Legend of the RMS Queen Mary*, was published in 2010, and is a popular seller aboard the RMS *Queen Mary*. *Spirited Queen Mary: Her Haunted Legend* came next, and will also be sold aboard the ship. Nicole is currently at work writing future books. She also serves as a writer, contributor, and correspondent to *Paranormal Underground Magazine*, and most recently writes for *Haunted Voices Magazine*.

RMS *Queen Mary* Research

Nicole has conducted numerous paranormal research investigations throughout Southern California and even out of state. Her favorite place to conduct ghost research projects is aboard the legendary RMS *Queen Mary* in Long Beach, California. Researching the *Mary* is an ongoing historical and paranormal quest for Nicole; she has spent the past twelve years investigating this renowned vessel. In addition, Nicole has recently launched her own website and blog devoted to the *Queen Mary*. You can find her site at http://www.spiritedqueenmary.com.

Media Work

Nicole has appeared in radio, print, television, and documentary film work discussing her involvement in the field. She also gives haunted history presentations about the RMS *Queen Mary* and other paranormal research topics at conferences and events. Nicole also serves as the California coordinator to the Oregon Ghost Conference, the Pacific Northwest's largest paranormal related convention. Nicole enjoys working with other paranormal researchers in the field, as she believes that through diligent research, teamwork, and collaboration we will all better understand the vast field of the paranormal.

Author Contact Information

San Diego Paranormal Research Society
http://www.sandiegoparanormalresearch.com
Spirited *Queen Mary* Website and Blog
http://www.spiritedqueenmary.com
Author Nicole Strickland
http://www.authornicolestrickland.com
Facebook—San Diego Paranormal Research Society
http://www.facebook.com/SDPRS
Facebook—Nicole Strickland
http://www.facebook.com/nicolepisd

PIERCING THE VEIL

Examining San Diego's Haunted History

Charles L. Spratley | $16.99

Many people search to find a good – and true – ghost story in San Diego. It might surprise you to find that some tales you thought were true, may be created from misconceptions, distortions, and even made-up historic events. Find the scoop here as some of the "truths" of San Diego's most famous haunts are debunked and stories set straight via historical research. Just how haunted is the Whaley House? Was "Yankee Jim" really hung on the property, or can this and other Whaley tales be demystified? Is there still a ghostly gunslinger's poker game going on at the Horton Grand Hotel – were the players real or not? The ghost story surrounding Albert Robinson and his burial and then subsequent haunting of Julian Hotel is disturbing – but is it true? The reality and history of many haunted places can be far more titillating without the smoke and mirrors, exaggerations, and fabrications. So pull back the curtain to find out what's behind San Diego's ghostly origins.

Size: 6'' x 9'' | 60 b/w photos | 160 pp

ISBN13: 978-0-7643-4140-3 | Binding: soft cover

PIER PRESSURE

California Piers from San Diego to San Francisco

Kathy Schroeder | $34.99

Travel along the California coast from San Francisco to San Diego and visit the many pleasure and fishing piers just waiting to be discovered and enjoyed. Approximately 500 color photos take you to 51 piers in the coastal areas of San Diego, Orange County, Los Angeles, Santa Barbara, San Francisco, and more. Revel in their majestic beauty as you learn history and trivia of each. Which pier is the most southernmost in California? Which pier is the longest wooden pier on the West Coast? And which pier, painted a unique green, can be seen from airplanes flying high overhead? Visit the Maritime Museum at Hyde Street Pier and the world-famous Fisherman's Wharf in San Francisco. Piers of all sizes and stature are found throughout these pages and will have you wanting to visit these incredible places yourself. This book is a must-have for beach, nature, and photography lovers.

Size: 11'' x 8 1/2'' | 448 color & 52 b/w images | Index | 192 pp
ISBN13: 978-0-7643-4353-7 | Binding: hard cover

GREETINGS FROM SAN DIEGO

Mary L. Martin , Tina Skinner, and Lindsey Hamilton | $24.95

Take a nostalgic, scenic journey through the San Diego of days gone by. 226 vintage postcards show the city as it appeared decades, and even a century, ago. From crisp Marine formations at Fort Rosecrans to casual strolls through Balboa Park, you'll see San Diego's history unfold. Dozens of images celebrate San Diego's red-carpet welcome for the 1915 Panama-California International Exposition. Romantic views portray Casa de Estudillo, where novelist Helen Hunt Jackson's heroine Ramona captured the nation's heart. Dodge trolleys and horses on D Street, ogle the glorious U.S. Grant Hotel, explore famous beaches and resort areas, and take in the panorama from Mission Cliff when it was an idyllic garden.These wonderful images illustrate sites that lured so many people to San Diego in the early to mid twentieth century.

Size: 11'' x 8 1/2'' | 226 postcards images | Price Guide | 128 pp
ISBN13: 978-0-7643-2562-5 | Binding: soft cover

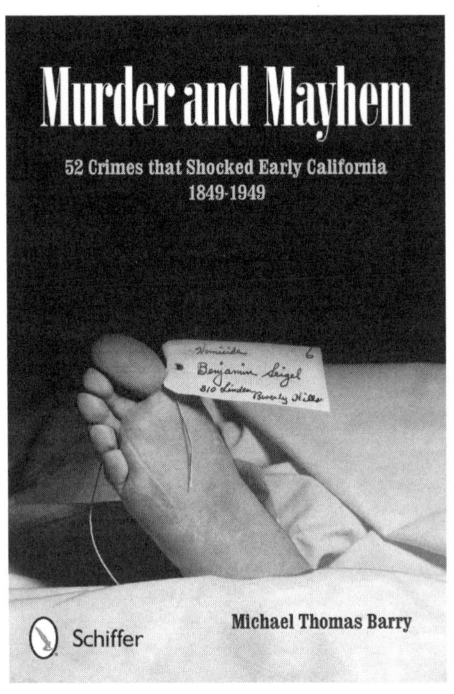

MURDER AND MAYHEM

52 Crimes that Shocked Early California 1849-1949

Michael Thomas Barry | $19.99

Relive some of the most notorious and long-forgotten historical crime stories of early California, from the Gold Rush to the mid-twentieth century. Told through shocking newspaper headlines of the time, these 52 stories include the exploits and dastardly deeds of infamous bandits, Joaquin Murrieta, Juan Flores, and Tiburcio Vasquez. Experience the poetic adventures of the most famous stagecoach robber, Black Bart, the murderous rampages of fiends, such as John Anschlag, Mose Gibson, Leon Soeder, Theodore Durrant, and the infamous Black Widow, Louise Peete. Also discussed are a treasure trove of unsolved murders including the notorious Black Dahlia slaying, the killing of mobster Bugsy Siegel, and the San Diego Slayer case. These true tales come to life with dozens of rare photographs. Sit back and relax as the darker side of the Golden State is explored.

Size: 6'' x 9'' | 87 color & b/w photos | Index | 192 pp
ISBN13: 978-0-7643-3968-4 | Binding: soft cover